MURDER & MAYHEM
IN
GRAND RAPIDS

TOBIN T. BUHK

THE
History
PRESS

Published by The History Press
Charleston, SC
www.historypress.net

Copyright © 2015 by Tobin T. Buhk
All rights reserved

First published 2015

Manufactured in the United States

ISBN 978.1.46711.752.4

Library of Congress Control Number: 2015947040

For Janet H. Buhk, 1938–2009.
Thanks, Mom, for all of those magical trips back in time.

CONTENTS

Introduction: The Cell   7

1. Midnight Express, 1885   11
2. Full Throttle: The Murder of Mrs. Mary McKendrick, 1894   27
3. The Murder of Detective George Powers, 1895   45
4. The Not-So-Masked Crusader: Reverend Ferris's War on
    Vice, 1902   65
5. "Auntie" Smith, the Abortionist, 1902   75
6. "Ghastly Exhibit": The Murder Trial of Mrs. Nancy Jeanette
    Flood, 1903   91
7. In the Bag, 1907   113
8. The Usual Suspects, 1921   127

Bibliography   157
About the Author   160

THE CELL

Please allow me to introduce a few recent acquaintances of mine: Joseph Morrison, a chicken thief who just couldn't stay put in the county jail; John Smalley, a violent train robber who gunned down veteran detective George Powers; "Auntie" Smith, a midwife by day and an abortionist by night; Jennie Flood, a widow with a get-rich scheme that involved a shotgun and an insurance application; Thomas Stockard, who ran the most notorious hotel in Grand Rapids; Morris Newton, who attempted to send a family secret to the bottom of the Grand River; Leo Bolger, who held the key to solving *the* crime of Prohibition-era Grand Rapids; and "Pearl Button," a bootlegger whose lucrative business ended with an empty bottle.

This is the motley cast of characters who live and die in the following narrative—an exploration of crime in early Grand Rapids.

It all began with a cell.

As a kid, I loved the old Grand Rapids Public Museum. My mom had a knack for transforming a mundane day trip into a magical trip back in time. We relived the world wars through the armory, said hello to the Egyptian mummies and then passed through the corridor and into "Gaslight Village"—a re-creation of a nineteenth-century street scene. As we made our way down the boardwalk, we passed the cigar store Indian—a silent, ageless sentinel of a bygone tobacco shop—and then hopped aboard the streetcar and pretended to take a ride around town, which included a pharmacy, a dentist's office and a mortuary.

In gaslight-era Grand Rapids, a horse-drawn trolley passes by in a detail from this stereograph, circa 1870–90, by Schuyler Baldwin. *Author's collection.*

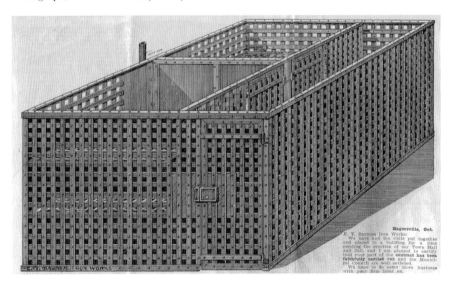

This lattice-style cellblock constructed for an Ontario jail by E.T. Barnum—a Detroit-based company that specialized in jail cells—is depicted in the company's late nineteenth-century catalogue. It provides a glimpse of a typical county cellblock from the era. *Author's collection.*

To a future crime writer, the most fascinating exhibit was the jail located at the end of the street. An empty chair sat by the desk outside of a single-bar steel cell as if a constable had just stepped out to puff on a cigar. A giant book containing mug shots lay open on the desk. As I peered through the glass at the thin cot in the empty cell, I wondered about the people who once stood on the inside of those bars—the villains in the story of Grand Rapids. (Today, the cell, along with a second "lattice-type" cell, is kept in the museum's storage facility. It is most likely a Grand Rapids original, although opinion varies about whether it came from the old Kent County Jail or one of the old Grand Rapids Police buildings.)

This volume is an attempt to resurrect the perpetrators who once inhabited that jail cell and the ever-vigilant constables who kept law and order in an era

TRIAL BEGINS !

Mrs. Calfornia J. S. Smith Faces Serious Charge.

CRIMINAL OPERATION

Is Alleged to Have Been Performed by the Woman.

Causing the Death of Bertha Van Norman —Ray Downer, Girl's Lover, Has Not Been Located.

A headline from the January 6, 1903 *Evening Post*. Bertha Van Norman's death shocked the city and publicly exposed the city's seedy underbelly.

INTRODUCTION

Abortion was a vigorously prosecuted crime in early twentieth-century America. Authorities in Oakland, California, offered the hefty sum of $1,000 for the capture of an alleged abortionist in 1919. *Author's collection.*

before the advent of modern forensics techniques. Each chapter recounts a single story from the sinister side of yesteryear Grand Rapids—most of them brutal, blood-spattered cases of homicide. However, to keep the narrative from becoming too serious, and to represent the full spectrum of criminality in the River City, I've also included a bit of mayhem at the end of each section in the form of an anecdote—a light-hearted yarn illustrating the sometimes tragic-comic nature of crime.

The following stories represent a cross section of crime in the River City from the 1880s to the 1920s and, to a degree, a scale model of murder and mayhem throughout the Midwest during this era. Dig deep enough into the dirt of other metropolitan areas and characters like "Auntie" Smith, Jennie Flood and Leo Bolger will emerge.

They are a fascinating cast of characters. I hope you enjoy meeting them as much as I did.

1

MIDNIGHT EXPRESS, 1885

The mystery, to all who know the men, was how they possibly managed to crawl through such small openings.
—Grand Rapids Times, *April 24, 1885*

Lorenzo Payne, a con man awaiting trial on a charge of swindling over $1,000 from various Lowell businessmen, kept an eye out for the night watchman as his cellmate, Joseph Morrison, filed away at the bars of their second-tier cell in the Kent County Jail.

Morrison and Payne, who occupied a double cell at the eastern side of the jail's second-story cellblock, made an odd couple. Morrison, at five-eleven and 184 pounds, was tall with a wiry, athletic physique and broad shoulders. Lorenzo Payne stood four inches shorter and tilted the scales at 137.

Thirty-seven-year-old Payne had fleeced Lowell merchants in a con game a few months earlier and nearly got away with it. He retreated to Detroit and hopped across the border to Windsor, Canada. He had been on the lam for weeks when he crossed back into Detroit on March 17. Lured to the city's bustling nightlife like a bug to a lantern, Payne spent a night on the town, including a trip to the theater, before waking up with a private detective's handcuffs on his wrists. He was dragged back to Kent County's secure lockup, where he sweated out the days until his trial.

Morrison, a twenty-one-year-old newlywed and a soon-to-be-father, was arrested for stealing chickens in early April 1885. He pleaded guilty and was awaiting the sentence hearing. He didn't expect the judge to hand down a

A sketch of a bar-type cell, also from the E.T. Barnum *Jail Cell Catalogue*. This type of cell, containing a door with a food slot at the floor level, is similar in layout to the one from which Morrison and Payne escaped in 1885. The cell bars Morrison filed through were lattice style of one-third-inch thickness. *Author's collection.*

harsh penalty, but the thought of spending his child's birthday behind bars horrified him enough to risk compounding his crime with a jailbreak. He chose the wee hours of Thursday morning, April 23, 1885, for a midnight run.

The plan had been days in the making. Earlier in the week, Morrison's pregnant wife had smuggled two lines of steel wire and a pair of red mittens into the jail during visitation. Morrison created an ersatz hacksaw by looping the wire at each end into handles. Using the mittens, which allowed him to apply pressure without lacerating his palms, he managed to cut through the one-third-inch-thick iron bars around the opening used to pass food into the cell.

The soft iron had given way easily to the two lines of steel cord. Morrison left just enough metal on the outside of the bars to elude detection by the guards. He also covered the scored metal with soap.

While Morrison finished the job around one o'clock on Thursday morning, Payne kept his eyes peeled for the turnkey. He suspected that the sheriff's men had caught wind of the plot because every half hour Deputy Burch tiptoed by the cellblock in his stocking feet. The quiet-stepping lawman apparently expected to catch somebody in a breakout attempt.

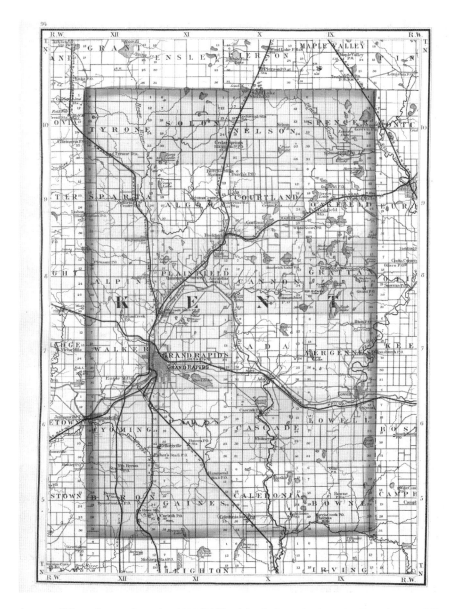

A map of Kent County from the 1873 *Walling Atlas*. In its early days, the Kent County Jail housed inmates from both Kent and Ottawa Counties. *Wikimedia Commons*.

After a few minutes, Morrison managed to saw through the remaining iron. He grunted as he forced the severed bars outward, widening the hole to approximately seven and a half by eleven and a half inches—just about the size of a sheet of paper. Payne squeezed through the gap first and waited in the corridor. Morrison passed a bundle of bedsheets to Payne and then struggled to contort his five-foot, eleven-inch frame through the hole.

The chicken thief, with the grifter on his heels, tiptoed to the end of the corridor. As they made their way through the cellblock, they whispered their farewells to the other jailbirds, including Morrison's brother Edward, who also stood accused of stealing chickens.

At the end of the passageway, Morrison went to work filing through the iron bars at the backside of the cellblock. He had done the bulk of the sawing over the previous few days. The guards, relaxed in their daily grind, often left the prisoners wander the corridors without supervision, and the dimly lit corner Morrison chose was barely visible from a distance.

The four other inmates in the second-tier cells watched as Morrison's arm rhythmically moved back and forth, creating an occasional spark that

The Kent County Jail is visible just beyond the bridge in this stereograph by Schuyler Baldwin, circa 1870–90. *Author's collection.*

glowed like an amber firefly before fading into the darkness. John McCairn, serving a fifteen-day stint for public drunkenness, smirked as he watched Morrison sit on the cellblock floor and use his legs as a lever to force open the five bars he had sawed. The two silhouettes then passed into the outer corridor, where Morrison began sawing through two two-inch-thick steel bars over the windows.

For over an hour, Morrison worked at the bars while Payne knotted together the bedsheets. The steel took longer to sever, but by 2:30 a.m., Morrison had managed to cut away two steel rods. They dropped the string of knotted bedsheets out the window and squirreled down to freedom.

Morrison went first, shimmying down the makeshift rope ladder. Payne threw a bundle of clothes through the window and then started down. Proving that there was no honor among thieves, Morrison grabbed Payne's clothes and ran off, leaving his cellmate dangling in midair wearing nothing but tattered rags.

Morrison crept along the outside of the wooden fence separating the jail from Pike Street and darted across Campau Street to Waterloo.

Kent County sheriff Lyman T. Kinney couldn't sleep on Wednesday night. Burdened by a backlog of paperwork, he woke up around four thirty on Thursday morning. Before beginning what promised to be a very long day on the job, he decided to take a brisk walk around the jail. He shuffled down the steps of the sheriff's residence, ambled past the west side of the structure and turned east. He stopped in his tracks when he reached the southeast corner.

His heart sank as he noticed the rope ladder of bedsheets stretching thirty feet to a second-story window. Kinney ran to the public entrance of the building, unlocked the door and climbed the stairs to the second story, where he discovered how Morrison and Payne had escaped from his escape-proof jail. At the base of the windows, at the spot where the knotted bedsheets were tied to one of the unsevered bars, he found the steel cable and red mittens lying on the floor.

How, Kinney wondered, would he explain to the press that two petty thieves had managed to escape from his escape-proof prison? Even worse, how would he explain that he had failed to foil the plan when he learned about it the night before from a tipster named Charles Blakesley?

While Kinney used the phone to wake up sheriffs around the vicinity, his deputies combed the area for clues. They discovered the getaway vehicle: a horse and buggy someone stole from a barn on Bridge Street.

As Kinney's men hunted high and low for Morrison and Payne, a reporter for the *Grand Rapids Daily Democrat* traveled to 29 Earle Street to interview Charles Blakesley, the man who had tipped off Kinney about Morrison's plot. Blakesley explained how he had come to hear about the escape.

A teamster who worked for the Grand Rapids Stove Company, Blakesley had a large load to move on Wednesday, so he enlisted the help of Byron Heddes, who had just finished a fifteen-day stint at the jail for drunken and disorderly behavior. The two men chatted as they worked. Blakesley ribbed Heddes by asking how he liked the accommodations in the city's most notorious inn.

"Oh, first rate. There are a lot of nice fellows there," Heddes said, before cryptically adding, "Something is going to happen soon."

"I asked him what is was," Blakesley told the reporter, "and after some hesitation, he told me that a couple of men, or perhaps three, were going to break jail that night, that they intended escaping Tuesday night but they had yet one bar to saw through and that they would get away either Wednesday night or Thursday at the very latest."

Blakesley suggested a call to the sheriff, but Heddes hesitated. "I was afraid they would murder me," Heddes said. "They threatened to kill anybody who squealed."

Heddes asked Blakesley not to say anything, and at first he agreed. He knew Heddes as a habitual liar and didn't put much value in the jailbreak story. But later that night—Wednesday, April 22, 1885—Blakesley explained, he had second thoughts and decided to phone police headquarters. The constable on the other end of the line, Officer John Quigg, suggested he contact the jail directly and gave him the telephone number.

Blakesley dialed the number. "Mr. Kinney responded," he explained, "and when I told him what Heddes had told me, he laughed and said that the fellow was lying but that he would keep watch during the night and make an investigation in the morning, and if there was any truth in the thing, he would owe me a new hat."

Charles Blakesley stared at the reporter. "Now, I want the hat," he said petulantly, like a schoolboy who had been promised a piece of candy.

In 1875, the Grand Rapids police station occupied the second story of this building. It contained just two cells, so most of the city's inmates served time in the county jail. *Grand Rapids History & Special Collections, Archives, Grand Rapids Public Library.*

When Morrison and Payne made their midnight run in the spring of 1885, the county jail was just thirteen years old and the latest stage in the evolution of a facility to accommodate the city's offenders.

For ten years, between 1844 and 1854, the county's prisoners were incarcerated in a dungeon-like basement in a building on Canal Street between Lyon and Pearl.

In 1855, a formal county jail opened south of Bridge Street. The two-story, vermillion-red barn contained a sheriff's residence and two tiers of cells. An under armor of boilerplate iron lined the thick oak-plank exterior.

There were no shower or toilet facilities; instead, each inmate received a bucket for waste and a daily trip to the yard, where he could wash with a coarse brush and icy water pumped from the jail's well. On dry, summer evenings, a sheriff's deputy would march the inmates, each shackled with a heavy ball-and-chain, to the nearby Grand River, where they could wash away the grime accumulated from sleeping on the vermin-infested straw mattresses.

Then, in 1872, the new Kent County Jail opened for business. Located on Campau Street between Pike and Louis, the new brick facility looked more like a fashionable home than a county jail. Indoor plumbing kept inmates

A bird's-eye view of Grand Rapids published by the Chicago Lithograph Company, 1868. *Library of Congress.*

The Kent County Jail, circa 1870, in a stereograph by Schuyler Baldwin. The south side of the building (at the left side of the photograph) contained two floors of cells. The jail's public entrance is below the tower. The entrance at the north side of the building (on the right side of the photograph) led to the sheriff's residence occupied by Lyman T. Kinney in 1885. *Grand Rapids History & Special Collections, Archives, Grand Rapids Public Library.*

inside the brick walls. Although the new jail was more secure than its rustic ancestor, escapes periodically occurred, which led authorities to line the brick walls with sheets of iron in 1884. This iron plating, jail authorities boasted, made the prison virtually escape proof.

The county jail held inmates accused of major crimes, but most of the prisoners were short-timers serving sentences for various minor infractions. John McCairn, who watched Morrison and Payne saw their way out of his cellblock, was doing a fifteen-day sentence for drunk and disorderly

The Kent County Jail in 1927. *Grand Rapids History & Special Collections, Archives, Grand Rapids Public Library.*

behavior. Two of his cellblock mates, John Miller and Charles Rice, received the same sentence.

During Grand Rapids' gaslight era, there were a thousand ways into the jail. Most short-timers wound up behind bars because they could not pay the steep fines meted out by the courts. For example, William Dolhen and John Killing couldn't pay the $5.35 fine for public drunkenness, so each spent twelve days in the county jail instead.

Frank Jones spent twenty days in the jail for "visiting a house of ill-fame" because he couldn't pay the lofty $11.29 fine; William Anderson, found guilty of the same offense, paid the fine and walked. Fannie Kingsley spent twenty days in the "ladies' cell" after a raid netted her inside a brothel and she could not pay the fine. Emma Smith, on the other hand, paid a queen's ransom of $53.35 for "keeping a house of ill fame" and evaded time behind bars.

In addition to johns who visited "houses of ill-fame," the women who serviced them, drunks who caused a nuisance and the tavern keepers who served them on Sundays, others faced fines or jail time for offenses that included, among other things, playing billiards on a Sunday. They served

$25 REWARD!

Dr. Fred Schermerhorn;

32 years old, 5 ft. 9 in. in height ; weight about 170 pounds ; light complexion, sandy mustache, heavy eyebrows extending quite across forehead; forehead very high ; very full under eyes, and is a Spiritual Medium. Left Grand Rapids, Mich., on night of December 2, 1888, via C. & W. M. R. R. I will …y reward of **$25** for his discovery and detention.

LOOMIS K. BISHOP,

Sheriff of Kent County, Mich.

A rare wanted poster published during the term of early Kent County sheriff Loomis Bishop, who served from 1886 to 1890. *Author's collection.*

short sentences alongside the more malicious inmates waiting for their days in court for rape, theft or murder.

The county jail served as the city's prime penal facility until the construction of a newer, larger police station in 1882 and another in 1892. The old jail continued its service but began to slowly atrophy. The graceful old building fell victim to the wrecking ball in 1958.

Sheriff Kinney cringed when he read the April 24, 1885 *Daily Democrat* article about the escape under the front-page headline "Sawed to Daylight." He blushed when he read one line in particular: "Once the improvements in the shape of iron plating on the inside of the Kent County jail were put in, it has been considered one of the nearest escape proof of any jail in the state."

The message between the black-and-white newsprint was evident: human error had resulted in the successful escape of Morrison and Payne. The jail, with security once touted as invincible, had been breached by a pregnant woman, a poultry thief and a con man.

Humiliated, Lyman Kinney did everything he could to explain his failure to the press:

> *We had locked up, and it was after dark and too late to make an examination. We hear of attempted escapes almost every week from the men who have served short sentences and have been released, and upon investigating have almost invariably found the stories false. I didn't take much stock in the story, thinking it was the imagination of a man who would not hesitate to prevaricate. But I thought it best to take some precaution, and I instructed Deputy Burch to set up and keep watch. He remained up until 1 o'clock, making occasional trips through the jail in his stocking feet, without seeing or hearing anything.*

The sheriff vowed to hunt down the escapees: "I shall capture the fellows and bring them back, and don't you think otherwise for an instant."

Lorenzo Payne felt a hand grab his left shoulder. He wiped the sleep from his eyes with the back of his sleeve and sat up in bed. He recognized the outline of Sheriff Lyman Kinney standing over him.

"How are yer, sheriff? I guess you have got me solid," he said with a sigh.

Payne leered at Kinney as the escapee pulled on his boots. He would not reach Canada as he planned; in fact, his grand escape had ended just a few miles from the city.

The gregarious grifter blabbed incessantly all the way to the Kent County Jail.

"If you had kept away just one day longer," he told Kinney, "you would never have seen me again. I was all ready to skip to Detroit and Canada today, and but for this untimely interference with my plans, I would have been beyond the reach of Michigan laws before another night had passed. You have been following me so closely, I have not had time to sleep or rest until night since I got away. I sprained my ankle crossing the GR&I railroad bridge soon after I got out. I had made my mind that if you ever got near enough to cry 'halt,' to immediately throw up my hands because I knew that you would shoot."

The sheriff smirked as he listened to Payne's account of the escape.

Payne depicted Morrison as the mastermind: "He planned the whole snap and done all the sawing and worked that night when Deputy Burch was watching us. I kept guard, and when we heard the officer coming, we got around the corner of the corridor into the dark. I tell you that was an anxious night. We knew we had to get away then or never."

Payne grew animated, his tone becoming louder and faster: "That Morrison, God damn him! When we were ready to leave, we tied our spare clothing into bundles and threw them out of the window. I had a good overcoat and an extra suit of clothes, but Morrison had nothing to speak of, and what he did have were ragged. He was the first to get out, and as soon as he struck ground, he grabbed my bundles of clothing and skipped."

Morrison, Payne added, had said he would go north.

But Kinney had a hot tip. Morrison hadn't gone north and instead had caught a train south. Two days later, the sheriff nabbed the chicken thief in Lagonier, Indiana.

By early July 1885, three months had passed since Kinney collared Morrison in Indiana. Morrison had spent the time in a cell on the second story of the county jail as he awaited sentencing. "Turnkey" John Platte could hardly wait; he hadn't slept a full night in weeks. Each night, he made sweeps of the second-tier cellblocks every other hour and tossed Morrison's cell each evening before lights out. Kinney swore that there would be no more escapes on his watch.

If the sheriff had one weakness, however, it was in his laxity with spousal visits. Aware that his married prisoners, following an adverse verdict, would say farewell to their loved ones for a considerable period of time, Kinney freely allowed visits to take place in the cell reserved for female prisoners on the second story above the main entrance overlooking Campau Street.

Lyman Kinney was about to learn that history sometimes has a way of repeating itself in the most irritating fashion.

Joseph Morrison turned sharply when he heard a key click in the cell door lock. He recognized the figure standing on the other side of the bars in the amber glow of a kerosene lamp: twenty-year-old Charles H. Libby, the circuit court messenger, who often locked up when Sheriff Kinney and his turnkey, John Platte, were away from the jail.

It was Wednesday evening, July 8, 1885, and Morrison was saying goodbye to his wife and infant daughter. That afternoon, Morrison had received a sentence of fourteen months in the Ionia House of Corrections for the theft of a chicken.

Libby, a slight man with the slim, wiry torso of a long-distance runner, stood outside the women's cell and peered through the windows while Morrison kissed his wife and baby goodbye. Such public displays of affection embarrassed the young bachelor, so he stood in the corridor during the private moment.

"Well, Charley, I suppose this is the last night for me here," Morrison said as Libby tugged on the cell door, which swung open with a metallic creak.

Libby shrugged. "I don't know whether they intend to take you away tomorrow or not."

"I would, honestly, rather die tonight than go there for a year," he said as he stepped into the passageway. Once in the corridor, he darted toward the stairwell. By the time Libby realized what was happening, Morrison had slid down the bannister to the first floor and bolted through the front door.

Taking two stairs at a time, Libby raced after him onto Campau Street and chased him to Waterloo Street.

Morrison noticed a train heading into the city. Realizing an opportunity to gain a few seconds on his pursuer, he darted across the tracks just in front of the locomotive. But he mistimed his jump and caught his foot on the point of the engine's grill, or "cowcatcher."

Collapsing to the ground beside the train tracks like a bag of wet laundry, he felt a warm sensation as blood began to fill his boot. He crawled down the railroad grade and pulled himself to his feet. He had to keep going if he was to elude the younger, faster Libby.

Wincing in pain, Morrison limped to Fulton Street and headed straight to the riverbank, but by the time he reached the water's edge, Libby had caught up to him. The young messenger tackled him, and the two men rolled down the embankment. Libby jumped to his feet, tugged on Morrison's collar and escorted him back to the jail.

The press hailed Libby as a hero; Morrison went, tail between his legs, to Ionia to serve his term.

Inside Out

Despite a few well-publicized escapes, the Kent County Jail was a fairly secure lockup. Deputy John Platte discovered, to his dismay one stormy summer night, just how secure it could be.

Adverse news coverage of the Morrison-Payne escape embarrassed Sheriff Kinney's staff, so in the weeks following the incident, deputies kept an even closer eye on their inmates. On a stormy night—July 4, 1885—Deputy Platte heard a noise coming from outside. Determined to catch the miscreants in the act, he ran out the front door in his nightclothes. The heavy iron door, hinged with a steel spring, slammed shut as Platte ran around the corner. Lantern in hand, he circled the building but noticed nothing out of the ordinary.

As he finished the circle and approached the front door, he realized that he had left the key in the pocket of his trousers. To add insult to injury, it began to pour.

Platte was soaked by the time he managed to slip beneath the awning over the front porch. He pounded on the door, but the rush of falling water drowned the sound of his rapping. Eventually, one of the deputies inside heard his shouting and let him in.

A *Grand Rapids Morning Telegram* writer, under the caustic headline "A Jail Escape," playfully described Platte's ordeal: "After a full half hour's racket, ringing of door bells, etc., someone from the inner recesses of the domicile came out and rescued the babe from the door step."

2
FULL THROTTLE

THE MURDER OF MRS. MARY McKENDRICK, 1894

When we were tying her hands she said, "For God's sake, boys, don't kill me."
—*Henry Prame*

The two men watched as the door to the McKendrick house opened at exactly 5:30 a.m. on Wednesday, January 17, 1894, and fifty-seven-year-old Miles McKendrick emerged. For years, the carriage mechanic had followed the same routine: after a light breakfast with his wife, Mary, he walked to work.

Mary McKendrick typically remained home alone. She owned a sizable nest egg, having sold some property a few years earlier. According to local gossip, the suspicious matron distrusted banks and kept a large sum of greenbacks in a white pouch she wore in her corset. She even brought the bankroll to bed, tucking the pouch under her pillow.

As Miles hobbled down the street, the two men prepared to make their move. The first man handed a flask to the second man, who took a deep swig. The second man tottered as he followed the first man to the front of the house. With handkerchiefs over their faces, they pushed through the front door.

Startled, Mary McKendrick shrieked as the first man rushed toward her. She clawed at his face, her nails catching on the handkerchief and tearing it away. "For God's sake, boys," she groaned, "don't kill me."

The first man grabbed her shoulders and threw her to the floor. He pressed his knees against her back while his partner trussed up her ankles with a length of cord. She flailed her arms in a vain attempt to free herself. The first man slugged her in the kidneys, and her arms dropped to the floor, allowing the second man to tie her hands behind her back.

While the second man finished hogtying Mrs. McKendrick, the first man shoved a rag in her mouth, in the process knocking out her dentures, which clattered to the floor. He then wound a tablecloth around her head. He twisted the cloth until it became taut and then squeezed, his knuckles whitening and his hands trembling as he held his grip. Mrs. McKendrick's body shook convulsively, stiffened and then went flaccid. The stench of feces filled the room.

The two men pulled McKendrick onto her back. The first man gripped the neck of her dress and yanked, popping the buttons, which rattled like marbles as they bounced across the floorboards.

Undaunted, the first man ripped away Mrs. McKendrick's chemise to find the white pouch.

John Quartell, a clerk for a local grocery store, flipped open his pocket watch as he knocked on Mary McKendrick's front door a second time. He drew in a deep breath of the icy cold air as he waited for Mrs. McKendrick to answer. Once a week for two years now, he had delivered groceries to the elderly couple, but he didn't recall ever needing to knock twice.

Quartell set the bags of groceries on the front step and glanced at Jacob Boynton, a delivery boy who had helped him with the order. It was cold, and they had other errands to run that morning.

He sighed and opened the door. "For God's sake, look here!" he exclaimed to Boynton when he spotted Mrs. McKendrick sprawled out on the kitchen floor. He nearly stepped on her dentures as he tiptoed toward her body. Quartell dropped to one knee and leaned closer. The piece of gingham tablecloth was wound so tightly around her head that her high cheekbones, nose and eye sockets were discernible. He glanced at the pink skin of her chest and watched for a second to see if she was breathing, then quickly looked away, guilt-ridden, as if he had somehow violated Mrs. McKendrick's privacy by looking at her bare breasts.

Quartell leaped to his feet, pushed past Boynton and dashed out the front door to call the police. Within fifteen minutes, Constable James Mooney was on the scene.

A horse-drawn police wagon leaves the newly constructed headquarters in 1892. *Grand Rapids History & Special Collections, Archives, Grand Rapids Public Library.*

The violent crime rocked Grand Rapids. It was the talk of the mid-sized town, and before long, gossips agreed on two prime suspects: Charles Macard and his friend from Chicago, Henry Prame.

The Macard family lived a stone's throw away from the crime scene, and Mary McKendrick knew the family well, often hiking the short distance to chat with the Macard matriarch. William Macard told investigators that a few weeks before the crime, his brother Charles and Charles's friend Henry Prame had come from Chicago. Prame, he said, told him about the scheme and even tried to enlist his help.

Charles Macard, detectives also learned, had a criminal record. He had spent four years in the State Prison of Southern Michigan after shooting his neighbor, Michael O'Hara, in a feud that turned deadly in the summer of 1887. Years of bickering climaxed when O'Hara lost his cool and charged Macard with a rifle only to learn the hard way that quick-tempered Charlie Macard was even quicker on the draw.

Macard always maintained that he killed O'Hara in self-defense, but a jury found him guilty of manslaughter. He spent a few years behind bars before Michigan's Supreme Court overturned the conviction and freed him.

Charles Macard knew the victim and had the type of mercurial temperament to perpetrate a violent crime, but he was nowhere to be found.

Since Macard had gone underground, detectives interviewed anyone who might help them bring him to the surface. The investigation unmasked Macard as a homely Casanova who hid his trysts with a series of aliases.

Pauline Dennim, a Chicago landlady, knew Macard as "Lacy." She told detectives that Lacy lived at her place with a woman he called his wife. According to another landlady, Macard and an unidentified woman lived at her Wabash Avenue house under the names "Mr. and Mrs. Shepard."

Chicago detectives managed to identify "Mrs. Lacy" and "Mrs. Shepard" as a married Chicago dressmaker named Ida Wood. The stunning brunette didn't want her husband to find out about her affair, so in a devious twist Macard had adopted her maiden name, Shepard, and used it wherever they spent time together.

John G. Stevens, who worked on the docks in Chicago, told detectives that he knew Macard as "White"—a pseudonym Macard had apparently borrowed from his sister's husband, Lester White. One day, White told Stevens about an elderly woman who distrusted banks and kept a large sum of money in the house. The job required two men, so he asked for Stevens's help. When Stevens rejected him, Macard turned to William Bennett, who worked for the Anchor Line Steamship Company. Bennett likewise rejected Macard, who apparently had more luck with Henry Prame.

Grand Rapids detective Jeremiah E. (Jerry) Darr followed Macard's trail to Owosso, where he found another of Macard's girlfriends, Belle Mehlenbacher.

The young beauty would provide Darr with a provocative and highly incriminating piece of evidence.

Ms. Belle Mehlenbacher adjusted her bonnet, folded her hands in her lap and stared across the desk at Jerry Darr. With a round face, milky-white complexion and thick, pouty lips, she resembled a porcelain doll.

Darr had to do a little arm-twisting, but eventually Belle agreed to make the trip from Owosso to Grand Rapids. She swore to tell him everything about some letters Macard had sent her the previous fall.

Belle Mehlenbacher sat up in her chair and cleared her throat. Her porcelain cheeks turned light pink when she told Darr that she had known Macard in both Michigan and Chicago. Darr wondered if she playacted as one of the fugitive's wives, but he decided to avoid the indelicate question. A few seconds of awkward silence passed before the pretty brunette continued.

Macard, she said, often spoke about Mary McKendrick and her bankroll. He had also sent her three incriminating letters. She burned the first two and sent the third back, but she remembered them well.

Darr jotted notes while Belle described the letters. In the second letter, Macard made the ominous statement that he expected to come into a significant quantity of money soon. The third, postdated after the murder occurred on January 17, contained some greenbacks and an order to "keep her eyes open and her mouth shut." Wanting nothing to do with Macard or his scheming, she sent the letter and the cash back to him.

After the pretty woman sashayed out of the station, Darr reviewed his notes. It now appeared that Macard, and not Prame, had masterminded the robbery.

All they had to do was find him.

Twenty-nine-year-old Henry Prame ground his hands together as a small crowd gathered by his cell at the Kent County Jail. Despite dozing on the train trip from Illinois, his head throbbed—the effects of too much whiskey the night before his arrest.

Police finally caught up with the fugitive in Libertyville, Illinois, and immediately turned him over to Grand Rapids authorities. Police superintendent Harvey O. Carr leaned against the cell bars, folded his arms and waited for Prame to begin talking. Jerry Darr stared at his suspect with an emotionless gaze.

Lines of sweat ran down Prame's cheeks, and he knitted his brows together so tightly that his eyes seemed to disappear behind folds of skin. Detective Darr recognized these nonverbal cues as signs of a guilty conscience and knew it wouldn't take much coaxing for the suspect to talk. He rattled off the various witnesses who had seen a man of Prame's description running away from the McKendrick place on the morning of January 17, and before he finished, Prame began to blabber about Macard's scheme to rob Mary McKendrick. It was all Macard's idea, he said; Prame was just an inebriated accomplice who wobbled through an innocuous plan that accidentally turned deadly.

A stenographer scribbled notes in shorthand as the suspect described what happened in the McKendrick kitchen that morning. He had helped Charles Macard hogtie the old lady before stealing a large quantity of money, but he swore he didn't know Macard had throttled her. In fact, he rolled her onto her back so she could breathe more easily.

Terrified, Henry Prame agreed to plead guilty to murder and testify against Macard. He wanted to clear his conscience, he said, and hoped his cooperation would lead to a lesser sentence.

Authorities posted a $500 reward for Charles Macard. From the information they managed to pry from Macard's relatives, he had left Grand Rapids on January 19 and headed west.

The bloodhounds followed Macard's trail to Chicago but failed to apprehend him before he went north to St. Paul. Detectives found an innkeeper who identified Macard from a photograph and related a humorous incident. When the innkeeper asked for a name, Macard said, "Oh, just call it White or Black or anything you choose." The clerk chose "Black."

Macard had made it all the way across the country, but his lucky streak ended in San Francisco. Recognizing the suspect from a photograph on a wanted leaflet, a local cop slapped a pair of handcuffs on "Black" and sent him back to Grand Rapids, where he would face a jury on a charge of murder in the first degree.

Macard's trial began amid a mid-July swelter that had transformed the Kent County Courthouse into a giant kiln. Spectators fanned themselves in a desperate attempt to stay cool as they sat shoulder to shoulder in the packed gallery.

The state's star witness took center stage when Prosecutor Alfred Wolcott called Henry Prame to the stand on Saturday, July 14, 1894. The courtroom was packed with women thirsty for the drama offered by the typical murder trial. A reporter, irritated about the lack of seating, remarked, "There were so many women present that all of them could not find seats."

A *Grand Rapids Herald* reporter described the onrush of female spectators: "They swarmed inside the railing, filled the two seats reserved for them and many stood up in the aisle among the crowd of court lawyers and general spectators. The summer girls in the pretty hats and gay gowns kept on coming long after court was called and the gallant deputy sheriffs let them in through the clerk's office."

As Henry Prame made his way to the front of the courtroom, several spectators in the gallery expressed their contempt with hisses and boos, prompting Judge Edwin A. Burlingame to tap his gavel.

Prame took the hot seat and waited for L.G. Palmer, the assistant district attorney, to begin his line of questions. He sat bolt upright and looked straight forward in an attempt to avoid making eye contact with Macard. A thinning hairline had created a long forehead that glistened with sweat beads, and thick lips gave him the look of a man who constantly puckered. With months away from the bottle in the Kent County Jail, Prame had been forced to sober up. The stress of the ordeal caused his weight to plummet, leaving him with a hollow gaze, an ashen complexion and jutting cheekbones that gave him a skeletal appearance.

He explained that he had first met Charles Macard in July 1893 in Chicago, where the two worked side by side as dockhands. He traveled to Grand Rapids the following December, at Macard's insistence, "to rob Mrs. McKendrick."

Spectators along the rail leaned forward, and the courtroom fell dead silent as Prame described the crime:

> *Macard took the cords out of his pocket and bound her and tied the clothes about her head. I held her down and held her hands tight across her waist. Macard searched the house for the money but did not find it. At last he came back tore open her dress and took out the money. She struggled to put her hands up to her face, but I held them so that she could not.*

Palmer stared at the witness. "State further what Mrs. McKendrick said when you assaulted her."

Prame wiped away the beads of sweat covering his forehead with the back of his sleeve. "When we were tying her hands, she said, 'For God's sake, boys, don't kill me.' I said we were not going to kill her but wanted her money, and she said, 'Don't kill me, boys, and I'll give you all I have.'" Someone in the audience groaned, "Oh!" causing several heads to turn.

"What was Mrs. McKendrick's condition when you left her?"

"I think she was alive when we left her. I thought I noticed her breathing, but she did not have any strength left to struggle. I laid her over partly on her back so she could rest easier and followed Macard out of the door."

Sam Clay, Macard's attorney, did everything he could to discredit the state's star witness. Clay's defense hinged on the idea that Prame, and not Macard, had masterminded the crime, so he devoted most of his cross-examination to Prame's recollections of the event. He wanted to catch the witness in a lie.

During a brutal cross-examination, Clay attempted to depict Prame as a two-bit loser and sot who lived bottle to bottle and whose memory of the event was blurred by intoxication. But despite his best attempts, Clay failed to shake loose one single fact, leaving the jury with the impression that Prame was telling the truth.

Prame's testimony had consumed most of the afternoon session. Judge Burlingame adjourned court at 4:30 p.m. and sent the jurors to the Eagle Hotel under escort.

The heat inside the courtroom was stifling when Clay resumed his cross-examination of Prame on Monday morning, July 16, 1894. Once again, Clay attempted to catch the state's star witness in an inconsistency. And once again, Prame rehashed the murder of Mary McKendrick, detailing the crime down to the tiniest detail, including her last words: "Don't kill me, boys, and I'll give you all I've got."

Prame's testimony matched the previous day's in every particular, so Clay next tried to impeach the witness by throwing suspicion over his confession. He wanted to convince the jurors that Prame had engineered the heist and, once caught, eyed Charles Macard as a convenient fall guy.

"Did you intend to kill her?"

"I did not."

"Then why did you not confess to the crime of robbery?"

"I was charged with the crime of murder and had to plead guilty to that."

"Why did you confess anyway—to get a lighter sentence?"

"I did it to ease my conscience."

"Why did you tell this story about Charles Macard?"

"I told the story because I wanted to ease my conscience."

Belle Mehlenbacher took the stand next. She testified that Charlie had once told her about an old neighbor woman who kept a large stash of cash on her person. She also described the contents of three letters she received from Macard, but when she admitted to burning them, Clay objected. After a heated argument, he managed to convince Judge Burlingame to toss out all evidence regarding the letters.

Sam Clay needed to somehow undo the testimony of Henry Prame, who appeared sincere, contrite and, above all, convincing. So he decided on a two-pronged approach: first, he would continue his efforts to indict Prame, and second, he would attempt to prove that Macard was at home asleep during the crime.

Clay outlined his defense on the balmy afternoon of Wednesday, July 18, 1894.

"It is true"—Clay's voice rose an octave, and he jabbed his index finger in the air—"Prame probably had an accomplice in this work, but it was not Charles Macard, it was not any man in Michigan. It was one of those Chicago bums. We will show you by credible witnesses that Macard was asleep at the time Mrs. McKendrick died. We will not go further and show, though perhaps we ought to do so, who was Prame's pal. Some pal of Prame's did it—and I'll call him Stevens for want of a better name. Stevens answers the description of Macard pretty well as to size, and Prame picked out Macard as the man to lay it to…as the man most likely to save him from some portion of his punishment."

The first witness to speak on Macard's behalf was his brother, Will Macard. As Clay anticipated, the ever-loyal brother swore that Charles was at home when the murder occurred.

During his cross-examination, however, Palmer exposed Will Macard as a liar involved in a scheme to engineer testimony for his brother.

Palmer focused his line of questions on a series of letters Charles Macard had penned to Will from the county jail and had hand delivered by Detective Charles Gates. The letters allegedly contained directions from Charles Macard to his mother and brother to bribe witnesses and spike the jury.

According to Will Macard, Gates acted as a go-between by delivering the letters. In mentioning the detective, Macard raised the specter of an officer on the take.

"Have you received such a letter recently?" Palmer asked.

"I guess I have."

"What did you do with it?"

"I gave it back to Gates."

"Did you get another letter from Gates recently?"

"Yes, I did."

"Purporting to come from Charles and asking you to make a copy of it?"

"Yes, I think I received a letter."

"Where is that letter?"

"Kicking around home somewhere."

"Can you produce that letter?"

"I guess so, if it is not lost."

Sam Clay's second chair, attorney Nathan P. Allen, stood, his face flushed. "We will not produce that letter," he barked. "You needn't try any of that deputy sheriff monkey business on us."

After a heated exchange, Palmer changed the topic to Belle Mehlenbacher. Will Macard admitted that he went to see her after his brother's arrest, but he insisted that he did not attempt to coax her with $500 to evade testifying at the trial. He also denied offering to put her up in a safe house until the trial ended.

Will Macard's denials fell on deaf ears. The session ended with the jurors scratching their heads and contemplating a coverup involving a complicit cop. Palmer had won the day.

Charles Macard didn't want to testify, but Prame's testimony forced his hand. His last chance to avoid a life sentence would be to tell his side of the story and hope the jurors believed him over Prame. Macard's turn on the witness stand came on the climactic final day of the trial.

Clay got right to the point: "Prame says you told him Mrs. McKendrick carried a large sum of money about with her. What do you say to that?"

"I never made such a statement to any living creature."

"Did you know she carried a large sum of money about with her?"

"The only money I know of her having about with her was twenty-five dollars she paid me for some work I did for her."

"Prame says that on January 17 you helped to rob Mrs. McKendrick. Is that true?"

"It is not. I was not there at all on that day."

Clay held up the leather thongs used to truss up Mary McKendrick and asked Macard if he recognized them. Once again, the defendant denied ever seeing them.

Next, Clay grabbed a swatch of cloth from the evidence table and approached the witness box. "Prame says you thrust this napkin into her mouth as a gag. What do you say to that?"

Macard shook his head. "I was not in the house at the time and never saw that napkin before."

Item by item, the accused murderer denied recognizing every scrap of physical evidence the prosecution had presented, including the tablecloth the killer had used to garrote Mary McKendrick. He also denied attempting to bribe witnesses by sending, through Detective Gates, instructions to his brother, William.

Palmer grinned from ear to ear as he approached the stand to begin his cross-examination.

"Did you hear the testimony of Mrs. Belle Mahelnbacher?"

"Yes, sir."

"Did you hear what she said as to your conversation with her in regard to Mrs. McKenrdrick's money? What can you say to that?"

"It is false—there is not a word of truth in it."

Palmer changed directions. He devoted his next line of questions to the letter Charles Macard had allegedly scripted to his mother in an attempt to buy testimony.

Palmer handed the letter to Macard and asked him if he wrote it.

The witness examined the piece of yellow paper. "I will not swear to that."

Nathan Allen stood up, fuming. "You are trying dirty work here." He jabbed his finger at Palmer as if it was a stiletto. "If you get that letter in evidence you will open up the rottenest deal a prosecutor was ever guilty of. We will show you up and don't you forget it!"

Judge Burlingame decided to let cooler heads prevail and called for a brief recess so he could examine the letter.

Charles Macard returned to his seat next to his attorneys. The case for the defense had come to an end.

After the defense rested, Palmer called several rebuttal witnesses, including Belle Mehlenbacher and Charles Gates, who now had a cloud of allegations looming over his head.

Belle Mehlenbacher testified that Will Macard had come to visit her the week before July 4, but before Palmer could continue his questioning, Clay jumped up and shouted, "Objection!" He did not want the jury to hear anything about an attempt to purchase Mehlenbacher's silence. This led to a heated exchange between Clay and Palmer, which Judge Burlingame ended with a few taps of his gavel. After a sidebar discussion almost audible from the gallery, Burlingame ruled that the jury would hear her story.

Palmer stared at Clay for a few moments and grinned. Clay balled up his fists and sat, seething, as the prosecutor once again began his questions.

"Did Will Macard ask you not to come here as a witness?"

"He did. He said he did not want me to testify in this case. He did not want me to come as a witness."

"Did he tell you to come here and he would hide you in his house during the trial?"

"He did. He told me to come here and he would secret me at his mother's house."

"Did he tell you it would be worth $500 to you to stay away?"

Belle nodded. "Yes, sir. He did."

Palmer next called Deputy Sheriff Gates. This testimony, Palmer hoped, would further cement the fact that Charles Macard had tried to manufacture favorable testimony and dispel the idea of any official interference or corruption.

"Did you ever see that letter before?" Palmer asked.

"Yes, sir."

"Do you know in whose handwriting the letter is?"

"In Charles Macard's."

"Did you see him write the letter?"

"I did." Gates then testified that he immediately turned the letters over to Palmer.

Palmer asked for the letters to be admitted into evidence as "Exhibit A" and "Exhibit B," but once again Clay shot from his seat. "I object to this kind of testimony," he growled. "There is enough of stuff in this case to show that the sheriff's force has tried to put up a dirty, mean job on Charley Macard."

Judge Burlingame decided to keep the letters out of evidence, but they would not go unread, either.

The next morning, the *Grand Rapids Herald* described the contents in a headline article.

The first letter, "Exhibit A," was addressed to Macard's mother and contained a request for fifty dollars to bribe witnesses. The letter writer claimed the money would convince witnesses that they saw Prame and a man who did not match the description of Charles Macard flee the scene.

The second letter, "Exhibit B," was addressed to Will Macard: "You are taking things too cool. We must have this fixed at once. We must have $150 by Monday noon to spike that jury. This jury must be spiked. That is my only hope. If I can't get this, I'm lost."

Eager spectators once again crowded into the small courtroom to hear closing arguments. Prosecutor Wolcott described Prame as a dupe of Charles Macard, the "soul" behind the dastardly crime.

"Prame has the blood of this murder upon his hands," Wolcott said. "I admit that. I do not try to palliate his guilt. But behind every deed there is a soul—and gentlemen, after a careful review of the testimony, I ask you which of these two men was the soul of this deed. Prame has the blood of Mrs. McKendrick upon his hands"—Wolcott's voice rose to a crescendo, and he wildly waved his fist in the air—"but the soul of Charles Macard is steeped in blood!" His thunderous voice echoed throughout the courtroom.

He walked over to the evidence table and picked up the bloody rag and leather thong used to gag and truss up Mrs. McKendrick. He carried the items to the jury box.

"Look at those gray hairs, the gray hairs of that poor old woman, torn from her head and knotted up in these bloodstained rags. God forbid that such a crime should ever again be enacted in this fair city."

The prosecutor's dramatic appeal took immediate effect on the spectators. Several women audibly sobbed. Others dabbed at their eyes with handkerchiefs.

All four attorneys—Wolcott and Palmer for the prosecution, Clay and Allen for the defense—addressed the jury, but Wolcott's rhetoric clearly had the greatest effect on the jurors, who left to deliberate on the afternoon of July 21. It took just over an hour to find Charles Macard guilty of murder.

Macard listened to the verdict without the slightest sign of emotion, which presented, according to an *Evening Press* reporter, further evidence of the man's guilt: "The indifference with which Macard and his friends and even his mother received the verdict evidently convinced many who observed them that they all knew Charles Macard's hands were red with the blood of Mary McKendrick."

A mob of the morbidly curious pushed their way through the corridors and into the courtroom to witness the final act in the tragic story of Mary McKendrick: the sentencing of now-convicted slayer Charles Macard.

Jail turnkey Ab Carroll escorted Macard into the courtroom and unlocked his handcuffs as Allen watched the spectacle with disgust. "What sort of damned show is this that they are getting up?" He snarled as he surveyed the standing room–only crowd.

"Let the prisoner be brought before the bar of the court," Judge Burlingame said. Macard stood with Carroll by his side. "Charles Macard, you have been found guilty of one of the highest crimes known to the law,

The final destination for many men convicted of crimes in Grand Rapids: the state prison at Jackson in a postcard dated 1910. *Author's collection.*

that of murder in the first degree. Have you anything to say why the court should not pronounce sentence?"

"Nothing I could say, your honor, would make any change in the sentence. Under the verdict of the jury you must sentence me for life. I will say I was surprised at the verdict. I did expect to be found guilty, but not in the first degree."

Burlingame shook his head. "I had not intended to make any remarks," he said, "but in view of the statement just made by you, I will say I was not surprised by the verdict. I think it was just and right. I will state further that you are the first person I have met who was surprised at it. The sentence of the court is that you be imprisoned in solitary confinement at hard labor in the Jackson state prison for the term of your natural life."

"Good God," several ladies in the crowd whispered.

But Charles Macard was unmoved by the judge's harsh words.

Rodney Sessions, dubbed Grand Rapids' thirteenth juror for his omnipresence at trials over the years, had watched the proceedings from his customary spot alongside the jury box. A reporter asked Sessions how Macard compared to villains of the past. "Macard is said to have nerve," Sessions quipped. "Better call it brutality and then apologize to the brute."

Charles Macard stood and grasped the bars of cell number seven, on the second story at the county jail, which he shared with convicted thief Frank Covey. He gazed at the sundowners pouring in through the barred outside windows.

It had been a quiet day for Macard as he awaited transportation south to Jackson. Ab Carroll had kept well-wishers away with a sign he tacked onto the jail's front door: "Notice—No visitors at the jail will be allowed to see Mr. Macard today." Carroll did allow in a gift from one of Macard's many lady friends: a bunch of sweet peas.

The same day the court sentenced Charles Macard—July 23, 1894—Henry Prame faced Judge Burlingame for his role in the crime. Without consulting an attorney, he pleaded guilty to first-degree murder. Burlingame, constrained to follow the letter of the law, sentenced him to a life of solitary confinement inside the state prison at Jackson.

Prame had whiled away nearly a decade in prison when a parole board reviewed his petition for clemency in 1902. It scheduled a public forum at the Morton House, a fashionable hotel in Grand Rapids, where citizens turned out to rehash evidence and enact a quasi-official retrial. Several key figures in the case—Judge Burlingame, Alfred Wolcott, L.G. Palmer and Philip Wendover, foreman of the jury in the Macard trial—all spoke in favor of a commutation.

The parole board consented, ending Prame's life sentence in 1902. He settled in Grand Rapids, where he lived until his death on July 4, 1925, at the age of sixty.

Will Macard faced Judge Burlingame in March 1895 on a charge of perjury. After a brief trial, the jury found the younger Macard brother guilty and sentenced him to fifteen years in the state penitentiary at Marquette. After three years in prison, he received one of five "Christmas pardons" meted out by Governor Pingree in 1898.

Hazen S. Pingree, governor of Michigan from 1897 to 1901. *Detroit Publishing Company, Library of Congress.*

Expensive Wallpaper

Mary McKendrick's distrust of banks likely resulted from a bank scam perpetrated on the citizens of Grand Rapids just before she was born in 1840. In all probability, she knew someone directly taken in by the plot.

In 1837, Michigan's general banking act paved the way for fraud on a statewide scale. The new law allowed any group of twelve citizens to open a bank as long as they met certain criteria, such as a pledge of assets for security. In other words, the bank vault had to have enough gold and silver to redeem the institution's banknotes. With just a handful of inspectors to police the entire state, however, banks opened and issued banknotes secured by little or no backing whatsoever. In some instances, disreputable bankers shared specie, which they shifted from one place to the next to dupe the inspectors.

The Grand River Bank opened for business in a small, wooden house on Monroe Street. Citizens throughout the city, including pioneer Louis Campau, deposited gold in exchange for paper notes. Buoyed by the phrase "Michigan Safety Fund" boldly declared across the top of each note, they believed the bank would keep their gold and silver for a rainy day.

They never saw their money again. When the bank went belly-up and did not have the specie to cover its debts, people lost their life savings. They were left with nothing but fistfuls of worthless paper. Many of them, like Mary McKendrick, never regained their trust in financial institutions and kept their nest eggs tucked underneath their bedsheets. Louis Campau, seething

A two-dollar banknote issued by the Grand River Bank in 1837. For years after the bank closed, old-timers attempted to purchase lunch or glasses of beer with the worthless banknotes. *Author's collection.*

with anger, created a lasting reminder to his costly gullibility: he wallpapered the cupola of his home on East Fulton Street with currency issued by the Grand River Bank.

For years after the fiasco, notes from the Grand River Bank periodically resurfaced in the hands of an old-timer desperate to exchange the curio for a cup of coffee. In 1892, one longtime resident purchased dinner at a Grand Rapids hotel with a five-dollar note.

3

THE MURDER OF DETECTIVE GEORGE POWERS, 1895

Where the ball entered the face, just below the left cheek bone, there was a ragged hole, large enough so that two fingers could be thrust in, and exposing the muscles and portions of the brain to view.
—Evening Press, *August 23, 1895*

Detective Charles E. Brewster, a Grand Rapids cop detailed to investigate the Fennville train robbery, knelt down beside the tracks and squinted as he looked at the footprints embedded in the black earth. They formed a point at the toe, indicating that one of the thieves—most likely the one who had stopped the train—wore shoes with soles similar to those of fashionable ladies' shoes, like the "Razor Toe," the "Trilby" or the "Juliet," that were all the rage in the latest Montgomery Ward catalogue. At first, Brewster thought the group might have included a woman, but the conductors aboard the train all agreed that the gang consisted of five men.

The night before—Tuesday, August 20, 1895—five bandits had held up the CW&M Express train en route from Chicago. They stopped the train a few miles north of Fennville. After they rifled through the American Express Company's shipment and took four packages of money, they held the train's crew at gunpoint and forced them to relinquish their valuables, including gold finger rings and pocket watches.

As soon as the thieves were out of sight, one of the conductors telephoned authorities with a description of the culprits. In addition to the fellow with pointed shoes, the gang consisted of an older man with a reddish-hued beard who appeared to be the ringleader.

News of the train robber with the pointed shoes traveled fast along the grapevine, and by Thursday morning, every conductor in the city was eyeing train passengers for men fitting the description of the Fennville rail thieves.

That morning—Thursday, August 22, 1895—a brakeman named Charles Ruprecht noticed two suspicious characters board a train fourteen miles south of town in Dorr. The older of the two men was a sinister-looking character with a black, wide-brimmed hat drawn low over his eyes; a dark beard; gin blossoms covering his face; and a leather satchel that he kept

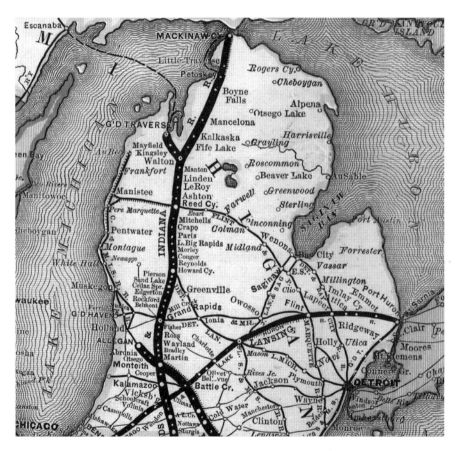

Detail from an 1874 Rand McNally map showing the Grand Rapids and Indiana (GR&I) line. *Library of Congress.*

tucked tightly under his right arm. His traveling companion was a younger man who was clean-shaven and also carried a leather bag. He wore pointed shoes. After watching the two men disembark at Eagle Mills, Ruprecht told his friends about them, and later that day, a railroad watchman spotted them walking along West Fulton Street in Grand Rapids.

The pair headed to the West Bridge Street Station, where they asked Grand Rapids patrolman Bradford Dean when the next northbound train was due. Dean watched as the younger man handed his satchel to the older man, who nervously hugged the two bags while his companion approached the ticket booth. The younger man pulled a roll of greenbacks from his coat pocket, flipped a few bills from the roll and handed them to the clerk for two tickets to Reed City. Dean wasn't sure, but the men appeared to fit the description of the bank robbers who had hit the train in Fennville.

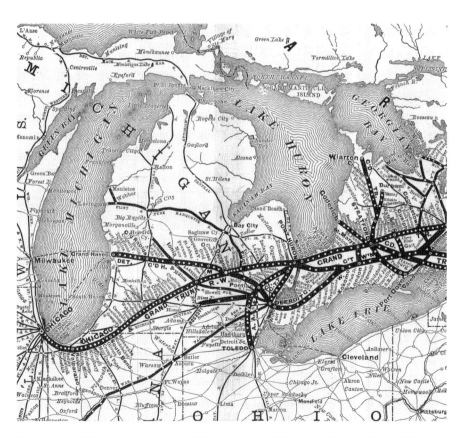

Detail of an 1887 map depicting the Chicago & Grand Trunk and Detroit, Grand Haven & Milwaukee rail lines in Michigan. *Library of Congress.*

The men loitered around the station until the train left Grand Rapids at 10:45 p.m.

By this time, word of the suspicious men had reached police superintendent Harvey Carr. He dispatched his crew of detectives—George W. Powers, William Youngs, Cornelius Gast and Sherman Jakeway—to the Detroit, Grand Haven & Milwaukee junction a few miles north of town to check all outgoing passengers against the description given by Ruprecht.

They hopped aboard a streetcar and managed to beat the northbound train to the depot.

Detective George W. Powers stood, his arms folded across his chest, and watched as the northbound Grand Rapids & Indiana train screeched to a stop at the Detroit, Grand Haven & Milwaukee junction a few miles north of town. The train had left the West Bridge Street Station promptly at 10:45 p.m. carrying two characters suspected of train robbery the night before.

Fifty-two-year-old Powers was a short, stocky man with dark, penetrating eyes and a bushy walrus mustache. His biography read like one of the sensationalized adventure stories serialized on newspaper back pages.

When the Civil War erupted, eighteen-year-old Powers left the family farm in Sparta and joined the Third Michigan Volunteers Infantry. He saw combat at dozens of spots on the map, including the epic Battle of Chancellorsville.

Captured following the Battle of the Wilderness in May 1864, Corporal Powers was sent to Andersonville. As he struggled to survive inside the infamous stockade, friends and relatives back home in Sparta presumed the worst and held funeral services for the fallen hero.

When prison authorities decided to transfer the camp's inmates to South Carolina, Powers and two comrades saw an opportunity to make a break for it. They hopped off the transport train. The bony, emaciated men stumbled into the woods and managed to find their way to Union lines. Following his escape, Powers mustered out of the service and returned to the idyllic life of a West Michigan farmer. After a few years of tilling the soil, he began an eighteen-year career in law enforcement that would span three decades. Throughout gaslight-era Grand Rapids, Powers prowled the streets as a constable working the graveyard shift. At the beginning of 1895, he earned promotion to detective.

His proudest achievement as a cop came in 1893, when he hunted down a trio of thieves who drilled the safe of Plumb's Mill at Mills Creek. As a lawman, George Powers was well respected despite the one flaw his fellow detectives feared would one day lead to his undoing: he tended to let his guard down in potentially volatile situations.

A sketch of Detective George W. Powers that appeared on the front page of the August 23, 1895 edition of the *Evening Press*.

As the GR&I train chugged into the depot, Detectives Powers, Youngs, Gast and Jakeway each chose a car to search. Powers picked the first passenger car—the smoking car, or "smoker."

Conductor William Stevens immediately recognized the silhouettes standing on the platform as Grand Rapids lawmen, and he knew whom they wanted. At the West Bridge Street Station just fifteen minutes earlier, ticketing agent C.H. Shirley had told him about the man with the suspiciously large bankroll who purchased two tickets for Reed City. Shirley then pointed out the man and his older traveling companion seated at the front of the first car.

Stevens didn't want to alarm his passengers or alert the suspects, so he tiptoed onto the platform. "Your two train robbers are in the front seat of the smoker," he whispered to Powers.

As soon as Powers stepped into the car, he spotted the older, bearded suspect seated in the first row.

"Where did you get aboard the train?" he asked.

"At West Bridge Street."

"Where is your partner?"

"Across the aisle." The bearded fellow pointed to the man sitting directly opposite him, on the east side of the train. Powers turned to look at the younger man and noticed a leather satchel on the floor between the man's legs.

Powers eyed the valise. "Is that your grip?" He asked, picking up the bag. The car lurched as the train began its forward momentum. When Powers reached up for the bell cord, the older man stood as if to give himself up. Powers expected him to hold up his hands for the "bracelets," but instead, he pulled a revolver from his pocket. Before Powers could react, the man raised the gun and shot him in the face at point-blank range.

The .44 slug struck Powers in the right cheek, ripping an inch-wide hole in his jaw and driving bone splinters into his brain before the mangled piece of lead settled against the cranium behind his right ear. As Powers slumped to the floor still clutching the leather bag, the elder suspect leaped from his seat and wrenched the bag from the detective's hands. The two men then bolted through the door and disappeared into the woods. In their dash from the car, the elder man lost his black slouch hat.

Detective Sherman Jakeway, who was waiting on the platform, watched in horror as the drama unfolded in the smoker. The scene reminded him of the "flickers"—moving picture shows that had begun appearing in old vaudeville houses across the country.

Jakeway had just finished his sweep of the second car when the train began pulling away from the depot. He jumped from the car and stood on the platform, where he spotted George Powers through the windows of the smoking car. Powers had his hand on the bell cord when Jakeway saw the flash of the .44. Without hesitating, Jakeway leaped onto the back of the smoker and went in through the car's back door, pushing his way past passengers who had jumped out of their seats and crowded the aisle in their frantic exodus from the train. Below a wisp of smoke and amid the acrid stench of burned gunpowder lay the formidable Powers, his face smeared with blood.

A brakeman named Fitzgerald, who also witnessed the shooting, darted into the ticket office to obtain a pistol from the agent. He gave chase, yelling, "Hands up!" but the men ignored him and kept running. He fired two shots but missed his mark with both.

Detective Cornelius Gast heard Fitzgerald's gunfire and took up the chase but lost the fleeing men in the two-hundred-yard thicket of forest surrounding Alpine, at a spot where conspicuously pointed shoeprints disappeared into the thick glade.

Within minutes of the shooting, a detail of six police officers was en route to the scene. By the time they arrived, Powers had regained consciousness and begun mumbling incoherently. He violently swung his arms as officers attempted to move him. It took four men, but they managed to get him off the train and into an ambulance. Someone found the black slouch hat and, assuming it belonged to Powers, placed it next to him. Sometime during the twenty minutes it took for the horses to run from Alpine Avenue to Butterworth Hospital, George Powers fell into a coma.

Police immediately organized a manhunt. The fugitives appeared to be heading north. Dogs in the area all began barking in unison at 11:30 p.m. And a farmer spotted the two men around Mill Creek.

Detectives Joseph U. Smith and Jerry Darr led a posse of "blue coats" that combed the

An unidentified Grand Rapids police constable proudly wears his cap, circa 1890–95. *Author's collection.*

forests west of the Grand River for the suspects. With orders to bring in the pair dead or alive, they searched throughout the early morning hours. Meanwhile, Detectives Young, Smith and Jakeway stayed aboard the train and, during the trip to Mill Creek, interviewed passengers who had witnessed the murder. They debarked at Mill Creek and backtracked, following Alpine toward Grand Rapids in the hope of cutting off the escape route of the fugitives.

Charles E. Brewster joined beat cops, detectives and train personnel in scouring the vicinity for clues. He discovered peculiar footprints zigzagging through the thick underbrush. They appeared identical to those he had spotted along the tracks north of Fennville. The younger of the two passengers, he concluded, had played some role in the Fennville train robbery.

Brewster also interviewed passengers of the smoker. Comparing their description of the shooter to eyewitness accounts of the train robbery, he arrived at the conclusion that the older man—the bearded one who shot Powers—was the ringleader of the crew that held up the CW&M train.

As the suspects fled through the forests toward Alpine Avenue, doctors did everything in their power to save the beloved detective. They wheeled him into surgery at about 2:00 a.m. on August 23, 1895, to remove the bullet lodged in his skull. Powers survived the operation but died an hour later.

Meanwhile, the manhunt continued throughout the morning and afternoon of August 23.

Wanted posters, based on Constable Bradford Dean's description, were distributed to train depots and sheriffs of outlying towns in an attempt to cast a dragnet over the area.

The elder man was described as "40 years old, full brown beard, rather dark, full reddish face, dark brown eyes, five feet eight inches tall, weight about 180 pounds. Had on when shooting occurred old dark suit of clothes, black wide rimmed slouch hat, brown leather grip strapped over shoulder. Talks in a peculiar jerky manner."

The younger man was described as "20 years old, smooth, square face, five feet six inches tall, weight 150 pounds, dark suit of clothes, soft black hat."

Back in Grand Rapids, Dr. Perry Schurtz conducted a postmortem. A gaping wound, the size of two adult fingers on the right side of Powers's face, had exposed the brain tissue, which was covered with thick, matted blood. The bullet had fragmented upon hitting the maxilla, splintering the brain tissue with shrapnel of bone and lead. Dr. Schurtz found the largest fragment—a misshapen lump of metal—pressed against the back of Powers's skull. Only the superb fitness of George Powers, Dr. Schurtz concluded, had prevented the lawman from dying on the spot.

That evening, while constables combed the woods around the north side of Grand Rapids, citizens read about the horrific crime in the local papers. The August 23, 1895 front-page headline of the *Grand Rapids Evening Press* screamed, "MURDERED!"

Over the next few days, a ragtag army of farmers, armed with shotguns and pitchforks, joined local sheriffs and railroad conductors in scouring the outlying areas for the cop killer and his accomplice. The search led to small-scale hysteria as residents eyed any mustachioed person with suspicion. A bicyclist who became stuck in the mud as he passed through

Dorr somewhat resembled the shooter. Residents watched in terror as the man, characterized as "a villainous-looking fellow" by locals, peddled off in a rainstorm. They waited until he was well out of sight before notifying the local sheriff.

It was the first in a string of false sightings.

Other "villainous-looking fellows" appeared across West Michigan. Deputy sheriffs treed two suspects in the woods around the village of Ada, but it turned out to be another red herring. Authorities chased leads in Cedar Springs, Grand Haven and as far north as Pentwater, but by nightfall on Saturday, August 24, 1895, they weren't any closer to collaring Powers's murderer.

Then detectives received a promising tip from McBain, a small lumbering community east of Cadillac.

As night fell, ex-lawman Gillis McBain, Deputy Bert Spafford and a posse stepped toward the veranda of the Brown farmhouse. Each man carried a Winchester repeating rifle. They were about to approach a ruthless character who, they believed, was the man who had murdered George Powers.

A handbill containing descriptions of the two fugitives had reached McBain the morning after the shooting. When locals read about the elder man who gunned down George Powers, John Ambrose Smalley immediately came to mind. He fit the description to a tee.

Smalley was something of a nomad and a figure of mystery. He periodically left for long periods of time, and when he returned, he had unexplained bundles of money. His reputation as a quick draw, however, kept nosy people from prying.

When in McBain, Smalley stayed with his wife, Cora Brown, also known by the colorful nickname "the Black Diamond." Brown lived in her mother's farmhouse. There were whispers that the Browns suspected Smalley was the mastermind behind a series of train robberies but kept their mouths shut out of fear.

On Saturday afternoon—August 24, 1895—Smalley arrived in town on the Toledo, Ann Arbor & Northern Michigan line. He made a beeline for a local saloon, downed a shot of whiskey and bolted.

Residents of McBain sent word to ex–Wexford County sheriff Gillis McBain that the wanted cop killer was likely holed up in the Brown farmhouse. McBain couldn't reach the Lake City sheriff, so he called Cadillac and spoke to Deputy Sheriff Bert Spafford, part-time lawman and part-time hotelier.

Spafford knew of Smalley from a previous incident. Two years earlier, following a well-publicized holdup of a Michigan Southern Railroad train near Kendalville, Indiana, Smalley had showed up at the American House hotel in Cadillac with a valise full of cash. A search of his bag revealed $1,700 in greenbacks and eight gold watches. Suspecting Smalley to be one of the bandits responsible for the Indiana robbery, the Wexford County sheriff contacted railroad authorities. Two weeks passed without word from Indiana, so Smalley was fined $17 for carrying concealed weapons and released.

The more Spafford thought about Smalley, the more convinced he became that Smalley led a gang of notorious train robbers that terrorized lines throughout the Midwest. A posse gathered in the lobby of the Hotel McKinnon—Spafford's business in Cadillac—and headed out toward McBain around dusk. They met Gillis McBain on the way and arrived at the Brown farmhouse as night fell on Saturday, August 24.

As the posse surrounded the house, Spafford and McBain crept up to the porch. The flickering light of a kerosene lamp illuminated six figures in the front room: Cora Brown and her mother, brother and sister; a neighbor woman; and—rocking in a chair as if he didn't have a care in the world—John Ambrose Smalley.

Under the cover of darkness, McBain crept onto the porch. A creaking floorboard alerted Smalley, who sharply looked through the front door to see the muzzles of two Winchesters pointed at him.

"Throw up your hands, Smalley!" McBain shouted.

Smalley sprang from his chair and kicked the door shut as he palmed the two revolvers dangling from his gun belt. McBain and Spafford unloaded their Winchesters, perforating the front door with bullet holes.

The others scrambled out a back door, one of them shouting, "Fire!" and blowing out the lamp on the way. Several tense minutes of silence followed.

McBain tried to coax one of the women back into the house to check on Smalley, but no one wanted to go in for fear of becoming caught in a crossfire. An hour had passed when McBain grew tired of waiting. He and William Van Meeter smashed through the front door with their rifles cocked.

Smalley lay facedown on the floor with a halo of blood surrounding his head. McBain and Van Meeter turned him over. Smalley's face was greased with blood, and his shirt was so saturated that it was difficult to discern the color or pattern of the material.

Smalley had been hit twice. The first bullet tore through the muscles of his upper arm before slamming into his hip. The second bullet entered the left side of his neck, piercing his carotid. The positioning of the wounds suggested that Smalley might have turned toward the kitchen when the deadly volley of rifle fire showered the front room with lead.

McBain pulled the two .44-caliber handguns from Smalley's holsters. Each gun was fully loaded except for one empty chamber. That chamber, McBain realized, contained the bullet that had George Powers's name on it.

The dim electric lights cast an amber hue over the backroom of the funeral parlor in Cadillac where Smalley's body lay on a table. Constable Bradford Dean, who had given directions to the two men who boarded the train in Grand Rapids, leaned forward and examined the slain man's facial features.

Smalley's face had sharp, angular lines, giving him the appearance of sternness and severity. It was, Dean thought, a particularly sinister visage and one that he would never forget.

The man Dean had seen under an electric streetlight sported a full beard. This man was clean-shaven, but the stubble along his cheeks and chin suggested he had recently shaved. Moreover, the deep brown color of Smalley's hair and mustache, tinted with auburn and crimson strands, matched the suspect's.

Dean was certain. "That is the same man I talked with in Grand Rapids," he uttered. "I would know him anywhere."

While Dean studied the deceased, Detective Sherman Jakeway examined Smalley's coat. He slid his hands into the pockets and discovered that Smalley had torn out the lining so he could palm the revolvers on his hips through his jacket. Many of the passengers remembered that the murderer had reached into his pockets just before the shooting.

After Dean stepped away from the table, Jakeway leaned over the corpse. He nodded as he examined Smalley's face. Although he had seen the murderer for just an instant through the window of the smoker car, he was certain that Smalley was the man who gunned down his fellow detective.

Authorities in Grand Rapids received news of the identification with mixed emotions. The death of a comrade trumped pride in the crack police work that brought a quick resolution.

While doubts lingered about Smalley's exact role in the Fennville train robbery, the police believed they had identified Powers's killer. "Everything points to that belief, and the identification is complete," Superintendent Carr gloated to the press on Sunday, August 25. "George W. Powers is avenged."

Others were even more daring. Deputy Sheriff Charles Gates applauded McBain and Spafford. Their quick trigger fingers, he pointed out, not only rid the community of a nefarious outlaw but also saved the county the expense of a trial.

"That beats a jury trial by a long ways," Gates declared. "It would have cost this county $5,000 to have convicted him and every officer handling him would have been obliged to have taken long chances with a fellow as desperate as he was. Those fellows who killed Smalley knew how to use a rifle, and I'm glad they did."

The young man with pointed shoes simply vanished. Residents of Cadillac reported seeing a person who matched his description ambling through town on Saturday morning. The suspect carried a brown satchel and appeared nervous but disappeared shortly after being spotted.

Citizens of Grand Rapids were equally vigilant. "A sharp lookout is being kept throughout the city for suspicious characters," wrote an *Evening Press* reporter, "and Grand Rapids just at present is a very poor town for any one looking like a train robber."

On Sunday morning, August 25, 1895, friends and former comrades of George W. Powers crammed the pews of the Baptist church in Powers's hometown of Sparta.

"Make a chain, for the land is full of crimes and the cities of violence," bellowed Reverend J.H. Maynard, his voice barely audible over the cacophony of sniffles and sobs.

The coroner's inquest into the circumstances and death of John Smalley took place the next morning, August 26, 1895. Train conductors who lived to tell about the Fennville holdup, bystanders who witnessed the murder of George Powers and members of the posse all testified as flies buzzed around Smalley's corpse. The heat was rapidly undoing the embalmer's magic, and the rancid stench of decomposition began to fill the room.

Both Elmer E. Rice, one of the conductors robbed at gunpoint during the Fennville heist, and Shirley, the Grand Rapids ticket agent, positively identified Smalley.

The star witness, and the most curious one to the reading public, was Smalley's young wife.

The Black Diamond cast a quick glance at her dead husband's body as she took her seat during the inquest. Beads of sweat formed along her hairline as she answered prosecuting attorney Smith's questions about her relationship with John Smalley and what, if anything, she knew about his business of train robbery. The *Grand Rapids Evening News* reporter sent to cover the proceedings was fascinated by Cora Brown's apparent indifference: "The woman seemed perfectly heartless as she sat near the dead body of her alleged husband, even going so far as to make a weak joke during her testimony."

Cora Brown explained that she had married Smalley in April 1893. She was nineteen; he was thirty-nine, previously married and the father of six. For a brief period of time, she lived with him in Pond Creek, Oklahoma, where he ran a saloon. He became volatile when he drank, which was often. Cora explained that she lived in fear of his sharp temper, so she came back home to McBain.

She insisted that she knew nothing of her husband's crimes and never received any jewelry—an explanation that seemed fishy to the *Grand Rapids Evening News* reporter: "On this point the witness became confused in her efforts to account for the possession of certain watches that were mentioned."

Although Smith could wrench no new information about Smalley's unidentified accomplices, Justice Frank Wright concluded that the shooting of Smalley was justifiable. He also concluded that the evidence proved Smalley took part in the Fennville train robbery and murdered George Powers.

Following the proceedings, Wexford County sheriff Charles C. Dunham traveled to Grand Rapids, bringing with him the revolvers that Smalley always wore around his hip—a pair of Smith & Wesson .44-caliber pistols. They were displayed in the front window of Joseph C. Herkner's Jewelry shop as curios.

The case against John Smalley appeared airtight; he would go down in history as one of Michigan's most notorious train robbers. But then, an unexpected development occurred when Cora Brown received a shocking telegraph from J.C. Anderson in Brinton, a community seventy-five miles northeast of Grand Rapids.

After reading about Smalley's death in the papers, J.C. Anderson rushed to the nearest telegraph operator and penciled a message to Cora Brown. John Smalley, Anderson insisted, had an airtight alibi—one that he could prove after conducting his own miniature investigation.

According to Anderson, Smalley had spent the period from Tuesday, August 20, until Saturday, August 24, in Brinton visiting relatives. Anderson spoke to a chain of witnesses who, he said, could account for Smalley's every movement during that period of time. He gathered the witnesses and brought them before the local notary public, who recorded their affidavits.

This alibi presented a convenient explanation for one vexing facet of the case: how the bandit had managed to move from Grand Rapids to Cadillac unnoticed despite the absolute curtain thrown over the area by police.

Anderson's legwork stirred up strong emotions in Brinton and McBain. Meanwhile, sensationalist reporters reveled in the new twist. Their treatments of the story created reasonable doubt among conspiracy-minded readers, who began to question the findings of the coroner's inquest.

Gillis McBain found himself in the midst of a growing controversy. The ex-sheriff's supporters applauded his shoot-first approach and viewed him as a hero who had rid the community of a gun-slinging nuisance. His enemies condemned him as a trigger-happy tyrant who gunned down an innocent man to collect the sizable reward offered by the railroad.

To no one's surprise, McBain condemned Anderson's story as nothing but wishful thinking—a postmortem attempt to clear Smalley's name. But others familiar with the cast of characters also came forward to denounce Smalley's alibi and the men who backed it.

A lawyer named E.J. Adams—a former justice of the peace in Brinton—didn't trust the affidavits. "I know the character of the residents of Brinton too well to place any confidence even in the sworn statements of some of them." At least one of them, Adams said, had a criminal record.

Conductor Rice, who stared down the barrel of Smalley's revolver in Fennville, also condemned the alibi as fictitious and stood by his identification. "Know him? I would know his hide if it was shown to me in a tannery. I am as certain about it as it is possible for any man to be."

Rice described every stitch of clothing Smalley wore in Fennville, including his black hat. When a doctor discovered a similar hat brought from the crime scene to Butterworth along with George Powers, Rice identified it as the one worn by his assailant.

Emmett Dietrich, a resident of Grand Rapids and a lifelong friend of John Smalley, also identified the hat. "It looks like the hat," he said. "I would not want to swear to it in court, but I think it is the same one worn by Smalley. It is the same shape and color." Dietrich placed the hat on his head and smiled. "Smalley wore it like this," he explained as he pressed his palm against the brim, "with the front turned up and the top crushed in. As I remember, it had a band on it, but I see the band is removed from this."

Even more damning to the Smalley apologists was the fact that Dietrich could place John Smalley in Grand Rapids on the night of Powers's murder. As he walked home from work that evening, he came across his old friend on Front Street. They shook hands and chatted about old times when they worked together as loggers on the Muskegon River.

Most involved with the case considered Dietrich's chance encounter with his old friend as an alibi smasher. Nonetheless, the debate raged on. Smalley's friends in Brinton stood by the alibi and pointed out that Dietrich hadn't seen his old friend in nearly twenty years.

Smalley's alleged alibi led to a wild rumor about a doppelgänger. This story had Smalley as the mastermind behind a series of train robberies. While his crew of five, including a man who bore a striking resemblance to Smalley, hit train shipments around the Midwest, Smalley ran around Michigan establishing alibis for his double.

"A perfect alibi has been undoubtedly proved, and the officers admit it," wrote one reporter, "but it is just as certain that he planned the entire affair and thus had a guilty knowledge of it. The startling fact, however, is the assertion made that Smalley has a double, and it was he who shot Powers…Meanwhile the coils are tightening about the double of Smalley's and his youthful companion, and when they are captured the entire plot will be laid bare."

Any lingering doubts about Smalley's role in the shooting, however, evaporated when authorities identified the man with the pointed shoes.

James W. Brown, cousin of Smalley's wife, Cora, sighed and gazed at C.C. Needham from behind the bars of the Allegan County Jail. Whispers of Brown's involvement with Smalley had led to his arrest. Needham, a special detective employed by the Lake Shore & Michigan Southern Railroad, recognized the sigh as the sound of a man about to roll over on his fellow train robbers. He shot a glance at John Byrne, a special agent employed by the United States Express Company to track down the $16,000 stolen during the Kendallville, Indiana train heist. Needham knew that the break had come in large part thanks to Byrne's shrewd investigative work.

Brown cleared his throat and began a lengthy confession. For the past two months, he explained, he had lived high off the hog with the stolen loot from the Kendallville train robbery. One of his partners—John Smalley's brother Abe—worried that Brown's tendency to flash a bankroll would give him away, so he threatened to seal Brown's lips permanently. Hunted by the law and harassed by the dangerous Abe Smalley, Brown decided to clear his conscience.

He, John Smalley and John's younger brother Abe hit the train at Kendallville on September 12, 1893. They dynamited the safe and made away with $16,000 of the United States Express Company's money. After dividing the loot, they went their separate ways.

Brown fingered John and Abe Smalley as key players in a string of train robberies. He described Abe as a sinister character with a series of scars chronicling his criminal career. At some point, Brown said, Abe picked up "a bullet hole on the right side of the upper lip, also a scar on his neck. He told me when I asked him about the scars; he said he got it last fall in a train robbery; where the robbery was he did not say. The bullet came out on the left side of his neck, about three inches under the left ear, leaving a scar there."

Brown last saw the Smalleys on August 20—the day of the Fennville robbery. At this point, the Smalleys had enlisted the help of a young confederate that Brown described as "19 or 20 years old. He was of a sallow complexion, dark hair, about five feet seven or eight inches high; would weigh 135 pounds; wore an ordinary common suit of clothes, and about a No. 7 shoe." Brown didn't know his name, but Byrne recognized the description as a dead ringer for John Smalley's nineteen-year-old son, Oscar.

It was possible that the Smalley clan made train robbery a family business involving two generations, but Byrne didn't believe the young Oscar Smalley played an active role in the gang. Just before Brown's confession, he had wrenched a damning statement from Vic Taylor, arrested on suspicion of playing a role in the Fennville holdup.

Identified by one conductor as the robber who held a revolver to his face, Taylor gave a statement implicating Brown, Fred Giezer, John Smalley and John's brother Abe Smalley in the Fennville job. According to Taylor, John Smalley and Giezer led the gang. Taylor, however, did not mention Oscar Smalley, although it was possible that Oscar accompanied his father during the flight north.

According to Taylor, after the Fennville job, the crew split up; Smalley and his brother Abe headed toward Grand Rapids, which ultimately led to the murder of Detective Powers. If John Smalley was the shooter, then either Abe or Oscar Smalley was the man with pointed shoes.

Needham and Byrne watched as Lena Brown pointed a bony finger toward the grass under an elm tree—the spot where her husband, James, had buried over $1,500 in greenbacks that rightfully belonged to the Express Company. Brown had interred what was left of his take in the Kendallville, Indiana robbery on the land of his boyhood home in Gilmore.

As Byrne jabbed a spade into the earth, Mrs. Brown cradled an infant in her arms. "You'll never get Abe alive," she sneered as she watched the lawman's violent thrusts. One foot from the topsoil, the spade struck something solid. Byrne leaned down and pulled a glass mason jar from the hole. He wiped away black earth caked onto the green glass and held it up to the light. He could make out a thick roll of banknotes. As Lena Brown looked on with contempt, he removed the bankroll, unfurled it and fingered through the notes. It contained $1,565.

Elated, John Byrne sat with a reporter and described the treasure hunt; Brown's tough-as-nails wife, Lena; and the desperado Abe Smalley.

Byrne had met some tough characters in his line, but Lena Brown impressed him. "She has the nerve to hold up a train herself. And you should have seen that baby, only three months old, barking for his grub! It is a part of Northern Michigan where there are some hard people."

Byrne was certain that Abe, not John, had murdered George Powers. "Abe Smalley," he said, "is one of the most desperate criminals this country ever knew. He has held up trains, innumerable; he has broken into no end of houses and killed a great many people—and I doubt if there is another criminal in America that can size up with him."

As summer turned to fall, sheriffs and train detectives hunted for Abe Smalley, but the alleged train robber had gone deep underground. Then, in November, they collared Oscar Smalley, whom they hoped would lead them to his notorious uncle.

An *Evening Press* reporter watched as nineteen-year-old Oscar Smalley, flanked by Detective Jakeway and Allegan County sheriff Joseph Stratton, stepped off the train in Grand Rapids: "His bright blue eyes are constantly in motion, rolling up and down and from side to side in quick glances that seem to express something of apprehension."

The long arm of the law caught up with the shifty teenager in Oklahoma Territory in mid-November 1895. Wanted for questioning in the Powers murder, Smalley was extradited to Michigan. Jakeway and Stratton traveled west to escort Oscar back to Grand Rapids, where he remained at police headquarters pending positive identification as the man with the pointed shoes.

The *Evening Press* reporter managed to confront Stratton on the steps of the Grand Rapids police headquarters. Stratton agreed to answer a few brief questions about his prisoner while Jakeway escorted Smalley inside.

"Oh, is he tough," Stratton said. "He stole a saddle and one thing and another out there. You might think at the first glance that he is not very sharp, but I tell you he is one of the nerviest fellows for his age that I ever saw. He's sharp enough, and don't you forget it."

"What does he say as to his whereabouts at the time of the Fennville holdup?"

"He says he was out west herding cattle. It is a fact, though, that he was missing from that part of the country for three weeks in August, and so far his whereabouts during that time are unaccounted for."

"Did you hear anything of Abe Smalley while you were in Oklahoma?"

"No. I tell you Abe is a desperate man, and I doubt if he is even alive. They say he carries an extra revolver concealed inside of his shirt, where it would not be found by an ordinary search. This, you know, would come handy to him if by any chance he should be caught. I don't believe, though, that he will ever be taken alive. The only way would be to catch him asleep or for several officers to get the drop on him at once."

Inside the police station, detectives grilled the young suspect. After exhaustive questioning, however, Oscar divulged no fresh information about the train robbery or the murder of Detective Powers. And authorities could not find a single eyewitness who could place him at the scene of the crime, so they released him after just a few days in custody.

Stratton had egg on his face. If the kid was guilty of anything, then Stratton had failed to find adequate proof or squeeze a confession from his suspect. If, on the other hand, Oscar Smalley was guilty of nothing, then

A quiet moment at the corner of Division and Monroe Streets in this stereograph from Schuyler Baldwin. On the second story, Mrs. Nellie Buckley ran a millinery. *Author's collection.*

Stratton had extradited a suspect without probable cause and, in the process, squandered county funds.

The hard-luck sheriff became an object of ridicule for Grand Rapids reporters, who depicted him as a naïve country bumpkin.

Authorities never did catch up to Abe Smalley, who simply vanished. James Brown thought he might have fled to Montana; others alleged that he relocated to the Upper Peninsula, where he may have lived the rest of his days under an alias.

"Sans Everything"

On October 31, 1895, a group of partygoers made a ruckus that prompted a neighbor to call the police. Grand Rapids police sergeant Dennis Millaley arrived at the corner of Monroe and Ionia at two thirty in the morning. He could hear laughing and moaning as he approached room number sixteen. After rapping for a few seconds, the door opened a crack to reveal the outline of a man silhouetted by the lights behind him. Millaley gently pushed the door open and brushed past the figure. His mouth dropped open as he surveyed the scene.

An *Evening Press* reporter, who characterized the incident as a "rare orgy," described the bawdy tableau in an article that appeared under the headline "Sans Everything":

> *Four human beings, two males and two females, each in a condition closely resembling that of Adam and Eve in the Garden of Eden before the occurrence of that painful little apple eating episode…Wine was flowing freely, jokes of an un-Sunday-school-like nature were passed with great felicity, and when the sergeant struck his iron gray head about the transom he was painfully shocked at being met with a gatling gun delivery of the most approved swear words.*

The foursome was dragged in front of Judge William H. Haggerty and made to explain the particulars of their "orgy." Earlier that evening, they had attended a "stag party" and decided to continue the fun inside room sixteen. After listening to their side of the story, Haggerty offered them a choice: they could spend thirty days in the county lockup or each pay a fine of five dollars for disorderly conduct. All four revelers chose to pay the fine.

4

THE NOT-SO-MASKED CRUSADER

REVEREND FERRIS'S WAR ON VICE, 1902

Diamonds, silks, laces, gaudy colored ribbons and gowns graced the police court yesterday morning. The wearers of them came in a crowd and the spectators…filled the room until there was hardly room for Judge Haggerty to squeeze in the justice which he doled out.
—Grand Rapids Herald, *September 20, 1902*

The young constable felt a tug on his tunic and turned to find a man, perhaps in his late forties or early fifties, accompanied by a younger man. A smile spread across the constable's face as the eder gentleman asked where he could find the nearest house of joy. The cop pointed his nightstick toward South Market Street. Maisons de joie existed all over the city, he explained, but several establishments stood within walking distance from one another on South Market. He personally preferred Nellie Brooks's place, but he noted with a broad smile that the gentlemen could have their pick.

The two men exchanged a glance, thanked the constable and ambled down the street. Unbeknownst to the constable, the men were not looking for a good time; they were agents of the city's anti-saloon league gathering evidence for their crusade against the city's purveyors of sin, and they had just obtained the final piece: proof that local law enforcement turned a blind eye to brothels.

The older man was Reverend A. Frank Ferris, the fiery superintendent of the city's anti-saloon league. His younger companion, peach farmer John Bos, acted as Ferris's chief detective in his campaign to sanitize Grand Rapids from unrighteous behavior. They had begun their crusade by investigating saloon operators who violated the city's liquor laws by selling booze on Sundays. Their trail led to people who peddled alcohol without a license, which in turn led to a chain of brothels.

Bos, whom a *Grand Rapids Herald* reporter described as "a tall, lantern-jawed young man with Ichabod Crane arms and hands," targeted saloons. He visited bars all over the city, ordered a drink and then left it untouched. He carefully noted the date, time, address and place in a ledger he kept. By Wednesday evening, September 17, 1902, the peach picker turned private eye had gathered "evidence"—which he defined as four witnesses to each illegal liquor purchase—implicating dozens of saloonkeepers and madams.

That evening, Ferris carried the bulky ledger under his arm to the county courthouse. The magistrate pinched the bridge of his nose and shook his head as Ferris ran his finger down the list of madams:

Mrs. Sarah Abbey, No. 251 Kent Street
Nellie Brooks, No. 205 South Market Street
Minnie Brown, No. 195 South Market Street
Lizzie Davis, No. 199 South Market Street
Josephine Emmet, No. 281 Canal Street
Maud Harmon, No. 205 South Market Street
Katherine Hinchman, No. 94. South Commerce Street
Hazel Patterson, No. 88 Commerce Street
Edith Rogers, No. 88 Commerce Street
Emma Rogers, No. 266 Kent Street

In all, Ferris swore out twenty-eight warrants: eighteen for saloonkeepers and another ten for proprietors of "disorderly houses." All of the warrants alleged violations of liquor laws; Ferris and Bos stopped short of going behind bedroom doors during their investigation.

From the courthouse, Ferris sat for an interview with a *Grand Rapids Herald* man. He placed Bos's ledger on a table in the room.

"I do not think," he began, "that the people of Grand Rapids know the conditions of law breaking which are prevalent, and particularly the constant violation of the law by the saloonmen. I do not believe that there are one-half dozen of the 192 saloonists in Grand Rapids but that are constantly violating the law."

He leaned forward and patted the leather-covered ledger:

> *The responsibility rests with the mayor. Personally, he is a very fine gentleman, but he is weak in that he shifts responsibility onto other men. I believe the police board stands in the way of reform. I think the chief of police would do his duty if he saw his way clear. The trouble is not in a lack of information, but in a lack of disposition.*
>
> *The other night I stopped at the police station and inquired the direction to a bawdy house. A young officer there seemed to take pains in telling me. Repeatedly I have stopped patrolmen on their beats and asked them the same question, and every time I have been told just which way to go.*

He opened the ledger and slid it across the table to the reporter, who flipped through it with curiosity, jotting a few notes as the reverend continued: "We are not after the poor saloonkeepers on the outskirts of the city who scarcely make enough money to live and could not afford to pay fines, but we are after the downtown saloonists who set the example of law breaking for the others."

The door opened a crack, and "Detective" John Bos slid into the room. He stood by the door, his hand resting on the doorknob, and began to talk.

"I come here from Kalamazoo a few weeks ago, and I have been pickin' peaches. Two dollars a day I make, and that's pretty good, but peach pickin' is givin' out and I heerd what Mr. Ferris was doin' and strike him for a job." Bos smiled from ear to ear. "We got four witnesses for every case, an I guess them big fellers downtown are kicking pretty high over what we done."

It became clear that Bos wanted to step into the reverend's limelight. He spoke with a brazen, self-confident tone that irritated the reporter to the point where he couldn't wait to end the interview. He asked Bos about his profession, and before the man could finish his statement, the reporter bolted from the room. He ended his article by describing his flight: "the reporter pried the man's hand from the door knob and escaped."

One big "feller" who didn't care to be called out in the city's papers was Mayor W. Willard Palmer. The same morning the *Herald* hit the newsstands, local police under the direction of special officer James Mooney launched a full-scale dragnet. They rounded up dozens of names on the reverend's hit list. By midmorning on Thursday, September 18, the Kent County Jail had become crowded with people named in the ledger.

In a curious spectacle, the city's purveyors of vice crowded into police court, where Judge Haggerty faced a dizzying array of twenty defendants, including J. Boyd Pantlind, hotelier of the Morton House. Several of the alleged madams attempted to sidestep their legal trouble with an interesting but specious argument. They claimed that since Bos didn't actually sip the beverages he ordered, he could not know they contained any alcohol.

Those spectators who expected a good show, replete with saucy tidbits from the parlors of South Market Street, left the courtroom disappointed. To Haggerty's relief, all of the defendants waived examinations. He placed them under $200 bonds, which each of them paid, and they went home pending their trials in Superior Court.

The entire affair affected households across the city. The city's respectable housewives began to wonder about the long walks their husbands took after church or about the late nights they spent at the saloons with their friends. The city's taverns experienced a sharp, albeit temporary, decline in liquor sales as many a married man found himself confined to a sort of house arrest with a strictly enforced curfew imposed by a Lysistrata-type ultimatum: either he would obey the house rules or he would no longer enjoy intimacy with his wife.

Thomas Stockard, who along with his wife, Mary, ran the Cadillac Hotel at 75 North Market Street, had been in the wrong place at the wrong time: facing a jury for running a "house of ill-fame" at the same time the Reverend Ferris indicted the city's police officers for turning a blind eye to prostitution.

Stockard's defense was simple: he pointed the finger at his wife, Mary, who had already been convicted as a madam and sentenced to a stint inside the Detroit House of Correction. She was the one running the "disorderly" portion of the business, he argued, and her conviction proved it.

His argument fell apart when several officers—including special officer Mooney and Grand Rapids detective Sherman Jakeway—testified about their interviews with the hotel's working girls, who fingered Stockard as more than a little involved. As soon as they finished with a client, he apparently had his hand out for his piece of the action.

During his testimony, Jakeway noted that the Cadillac Hotel was not by any means the only one of its kind in Grand Rapids. He identified an address on South Market Street as a "disorderly house" run by a madam named "Dollie Moore." Since Moore's name did not appear on the reverend's list of warrants, Jakeway's testimony implied that the city's sin industry extended far beyond Bos's ledger—a message not lost on Superior Court judge Richard L. Newnham.

It took just ninety minutes on Tuesday, September 23, for the jury to find Stockard guilty as charged. Judge Newnham scheduled sentencing for Thursday, September 25.

In the interim—on the morning of September 24, 1902—Newnham faced Shaddrick T. Newson, a druggist who pleaded guilty to selling liquor without a license from his pharmacy on Cherry Street. By exposing the epidemic of liquor law violations, Reverend Ferris's ad hoc investigation placed anyone remotely involved with the selling of sin under more scrutiny than ever before.

Newnham asked Newson if he had anything to say, and the druggist simply shook his head.

"The offense of which you have been convicted, on your own plea of guilty, Mr. Newson," the judge said with disgust evident in his tone, "is one which society demands shall receive attention. This is not your first offense. Twice you have been before me for sentence on similar charges. Once the clemency of the court was exercised to give you another chance, and once you were let off with a fine. This time I am determined you shall undergo a more severe penalty."

Newnham fined Newson $100 or, if he couldn't pay, ninety days in jail. The druggist didn't have the money, so he did the time instead.

On Thursday afternoon, Thomas Stockard received his sentence. He stood and faced the judge.

Judge Newnham asked Stockard if the accused had anything to say on his own behalf before he passed sentence, which led to an interesting exchange that spelled doom for the city's prostitutes.

"I have only this to say," Stockard whimpered, "that I am innocent of the charge against me."

After shaking his head, Judge Newnham said, "In the verdict of the jury I fully concur. How any man can stand up and say he is innocent while as guilty as you unquestionably are is more than I can see. You have been convicted of keeping, with your wife, the most disreputable place in the city of Grand Rapids and must expect severe punishment."

Newnham, irritated by Ferris's story about a constable who pointed out the way to a house of prostitution, wanted to send a strong message to the pimps and madams running the city's maisons de joie and city officials who did nothing about it. He sentenced Stockard to three years of hard labor and then, in a rare gesture, addressed Prosecutor William Brown.

"Mr. Prosecutor," he said, pointing his gavel at Brown, "I wish to say to you that this Cadillac Hotel is not the only place of this character in the city, and where testimony is given in court it is the duty of the prosecutor and the authorities to bring the offenders to justice, and I sincerely hope that it will be done."

While fallen angels all over Grand Rapids picked up their wings and flew back to legitimate occupations, police escorted Thomas Stockard to Jackson.

The sensational trials expected by the public never materialized. The defendants received sentences similar to that of Shaddrick Newson. Some anted up princely ransoms to the city; others, who couldn't afford to pay, did short stints behind bars. Then it was back to business as usual.

And despite the efforts of Reverend Ferris, business boomed. The list of madams published in the newspapers provided a virtual roadmap to the city's vice hot spots. Bordello clients sipped cocktails as they flirted with the establishment's "inmates," and barflies downed shots of whiskey and glasses of beer in corner bars. But proprietors, thanks to the reverend's crusade, thought twice about serving liquor on Sundays.

Stories about the reverend's crusade vanished from the news, pushed from the front pages by an even more shocking and sensational case that would captivate the citizens of Grand Rapids. The same afternoon that a cell door closed on Shaddrick Newson, the death of a sixteen-year-old would expose a shadowy figure known to the working girls as "Auntie" Smith.

Judge Newnham's stern statement to William Brown and Reverend Ferris's not-so-subtle indictment hinted that the prosecutor's office did not do enough to stop vice in Grand Rapids. They may have been right.

In the last six months of 1902—even after Ferris's crusade—Brown prosecuted just one defendant on a charge of running a "house of ill fame" (Thomas Stockard) and just one for keeping a tavern open on Sunday. The other cases never went to trial. In the end, all of Reverend Ferris's hard work amounted to increased revenue for the City of Grand Rapids in the form of fines.

This did not mean that the prosecutor was soft on crime. In addition to the usual suspects—thieves, con men, vandals, abusers and embezzlers—Brown successfully prosecuted all sorts of offenders during the same time frame. These wrongdoers included five individuals for "illegitimate parentage," another five for "non-support," eight for "keeping gaming tables," five for "intoxication," one for "sodomy" and one for violating the state's "plumbing act."

While citizens may have thought twice about doing their own plumbing, bordello operators didn't; horizontal drilling operations recommenced on South Market and Commerce Streets.

MUGGED BY A MUG SHOT

It was an overcast day in August 1901 when con men W.N. Devine and William C. Lane, the latter wearing a black, broad-brimmed hat, stepped off the train in Grand Rapids to find a special greeting party led by Detectives Joseph U. Smith and Sherman Jakeway. Smith knew the men as expert grifters and had received a tip that they were about to get a game going in Grand Rapids. As soon as Lane stepped off the train, Smith noticed his black hat.

Ignoring the revolver at Devine's hip, the two cops escorted the duo straight from Union Depot to police headquarters.

Lane kept up his ruse as a legitimate businessman. "I work for one of the largest boiler manufacturing concerns in the county, and you will suffer for this outrage, sir," he huffed. "I won't be locked up like a criminal, and if you insist, you will do so at your own peril and will have to take the chances."

Chief Carr smiled. "All right, old man, just as soon take a chance at you as anyone." He threw the two men into a cell until Lane cooled off. Then he brought them to the Bertillon Department.

Mr. Frederick W. Weber, a clerk who doubled as the police photographer, snapped mug shots. Lane peered at the camera with his signature glare—a stolid gaze that some characterized as "icy." He wore his black hat tilted slightly to one side and retained the indignant expression of a wronged man. When Weber finished, a two-man detail took a series of measurements that included height, head length and wingspan. In the days before fingerprint classification, these measurements helped law enforcement identify suspects. A card containing these numbers along with two photographs, frontal and profile views, were placed in the "rogues' gallery"—a cabinet of cards containing the mug shots of suspicious and wanted persons.

After the procedure, Smith and Jakeway escorted Devine and Lane straight to Union Depot. Smith watched the two men board the next outbound train and eyed the locomotive until it passed out of sight.

The booking entry for infamous con man William Lane, compiled after his arrest at Union Station in August 1901. For stepping off the train in Grand Rapids, where he planned to run a confidence game, Lane was given a sentence of "hours to leave." A pair of photographs—front and profile views—accompanied by a series of measurements formed the basis of a classification and identification scheme developed by French criminologist Alphonse Bertillon. The "Bertillon Department" of Grand Rapids used the information from this rap sheet to create a two-sided card for use in rogues' galleries across the Midwest. This picture, by Grand Rapids police photographer Frederick W. Weber, ultimately led to Lane's apprehension in Illinois. *Collections of the Grand Rapids Public Museum.*

Their preemptive measure paid off. Lane got into all sorts of mayhem, which included a bank heist in Abington, Illinois.

By early 1903, he had gangs of detectives on his trail. Copies of Weber's photographs became fixtures at rogues' galleries in police stations throughout the Midwest. It was only a matter of time before some alert cop recognized him.

The long arm of the law finally caught up with Lane in Quincy, Illinois, when a young officer became suspicious of "Doc Butler," a wealthy cattleman from Texas who was throwing money all over town. After checking the local rogues' gallery, he realized that "Doc Butler" was actually William Lane, a con man wanted in several states. Six officers burst into a theater where Lane had just finished watching a play called *Tracy the Outlaw*.

The handsome mugger was mugged by a mug shot, courtesy of Mr. Weber and the Grand Rapids Bertillon Department.

5
"AUNTIE" SMITH, THE ABORTIONIST, 1902

The trial is creating more interest than anything which has come up in the superior court for many months and the court room was crowded all day, the space inside the railing being filled with ladies.
—Grand Rapids Herald, *January 7, 1903*

R ay Downer looked nervous. Sweat ran down his cheeks as he asked his landlady, Lydia Beebe, for a bucket of hot water. He explained that "Auntie" Smith, an elderly woman who had come to visit Bertha Downer a few minutes earlier, needed the water.

For about a week, Downer and his sixteen-year-old girlfriend had been living as husband and wife in Beebe's back room. The elderly matron didn't want to rent the tiny, closet-sized room, but the Downers seemed desperate, so she relented.

Beebe handed Downer a bucket, and he darted off, taking the stairs two at a time. Mrs. Beebe winced as she watched droplets of hot water, like a light rainfall, spill from the bucket onto the stair runner.

Bertha felt her heart race. Sweat beads formed on her forehead as Ray sat next to her, and all of a sudden, she became conscious that she was whimpering. "Auntie" Smith patted the girl's hand, smiled and spoke in a gentle, reassuring voice.

"Auntie" removed a swatch of cloth and a brown bottle from her bag. She doused the cloth with chloroform and gently pressed it against Bertha's lips. She brushed strands of sweat-soaked hair from her patient's forehead as she waited for the drug to take effect. Bertha's eyelids fluttered and glazed over.

"Good," Smith nodded as Bertha fell into a deep slumber. She reached into her bag and removed a tenaculum, a device used to dilate the womb. She tested the device by slipping her fingers inside the grips and pressing, which caused the blades to fan out with a metallic snipping sound that made Ray Downer flinch. Girls typically panicked at the sight of the instrument, so Smith had learned over the years to keep these things out of sight until her patients slipped into unconsciousness.

"Auntie" raised Bertha's nightdress, slid the tenaculum inside her vagina and gently squeezed the handles, slowly dilating the cervix. Ray Downer uncomfortably shifted his weight from one foot to the other as he watched Smith insert the spoon-shaped curette. Her head bobbed and her arm moved rhythmically as she worked. Ray began to wretch as he watched the blood-streaked hand dump what looked like an oversized clot into the slop pail. *Thunk!*—the crimson dollop struck the bottom of the bucket, making a hollow metallic sound.

Twenty minutes later, "Auntie" Smith waltzed through the front parlor, smiling at the landlady on her way through the front door. Ray Downer followed her down the stairs and handed the bucket to Mrs. Beebe.

Lydia Beebe peered into the bucket and saw what looked like a bloody chicken gizzard with a long appendage attached to it. Mrs. Downer, she knew, loved chicken, so she thought that "Auntie" had brought her a chicken to slaughter. She took the bucket into the front yard, tossed out the contents and then washed it clean with water from the nearest hydrant. When she returned to the house, the small pile of bloody remains had disappeared from the front yard—an easy meal for one of the neighborhood's stray dogs or cats.

"AUNTIE" SMITH, THE ABORTIONIST, 1902

A week later, Lydia Beebe watched with curiosity as Downer rushed through the front door followed by a bespectacled man carrying a medical bag. Twenty minutes later, the two men emerged. In his arms, Downer carried what looked like a bundle of bloodstained clothes with the ashen, sallow face of the girl she knew as Bertha Downer in the center.

Overwhelmed with curiosity, Mrs. Beebe peered through the open door of her back room. She winced. The room looked as if someone had butchered a cow in it. The comforter and bedsheets were completely saturated with blood.

Mrs. Beebe gasped as she realized what had taken place in her back room. She thought about the chicken gizzard in the slop bucket.

Sixteen-year-old Bertha Van Norman's eyes widened when Dr. Frank. J. Lee said that sometime that night—Wednesday, September 24, 1902—she would die. He could no longer help her, but he could help other girls by preventing the culprit who had performed the "criminal operation" on Bertha. He needed a name.

Bertha refused to divulge the name of the doctor who had performed the abortion.

Over the past week, Dr. Lee had done everything he could to save the girl. The previous Thursday, a young man named Ray Downer, frantic, insisted that he come to her bedside at a South Division Street address. Dr. Lee found Bertha in bed, curled into a fetal position, with a temperature of 104 and a pulse of 140. A pile of blood-soaked bedclothes verified Lee's suspicion: Bertha had undergone a "criminal operation"—a back-alley abortion that had led to a life-threatening case of blood poisoning.

He ordered her immediate transfer to the UBA Hospital, where he did emergency surgery in a vain attempt to save the girl. He gave her some ether, dilated her womb and removed a large portion of afterbirth. But Bertha's condition only worsened. Angry that a doctor's dirty scalpel would end such a young girl's life, Dr. Lee vowed to bring the physician to justice, but Bertha ignored his pleas and refused to give up the name of her abortionist. When Dr. Lee told her that she would not recover, Bertha decided to clear her conscience.

Her mother, Beatrice Burrows, sat on the edge of the cot, wiped a few strands of sweat-soaked hair from Bertha's forehead and pressed a cold washcloth over the girl's eyes.

The UBA Hospital where Bertha Van Norman died, as it appeared on a postcard dated 1906. *Author's collection.*

Bertha gripped the bedsheets with all of her remaining strength and squeezed until her knuckles turned white. Three days of incessant vomiting and diarrhea had drained all of the color from her face and left her with barely enough energy to lift her arms. The pain in her lower stomach had become so acute that she struggled to piece together a coherent sentence in between gasps. The result was a sequence of whispered syllables strung together one piece at a time.

Two other ladies in the room, a nurse and a friend of the family, stood on either side of the bed and listened as Bertha described her undoing—a romance with a man named Ray Downer.

Bertha's parents split when she was a little girl. Her mother remained in Grand Rapids, struggling to make ends meet, while her father worked north of the city. Economic hardship had caused Bertha to leave her mother's home on Bridge Street and move into a boardinghouse on Ottawa. From Ottawa, she drifted to a boardinghouse on Scribner, where she worked as a domestic in exchange for room and board. While there, she met twenty-two-year-old Ray Downer, a fellow boarder who worked for the Grand Rapids Brass Company.

For Bertha, it was a like a fairy tale romance. Then, in July 1902, she became sick while helping Ray's sixty-six-year-old mother, Minnie, with the season's canning. At first, she thought she had eaten some spoiled food, but when the illness persisted, she realized she was pregnant.

Downer insisted on marrying Bertha right away, but Bertha hesitated. She wanted to visit a doctor who, she'd heard, had helped other girls in trouble. Despite Downer's objections, Bertha called on Dr. Jennie Smith, known to working girls as "Auntie."

On Thursday, September 18, "Auntie" Smith walked into the boardinghouse at 232 South Division Street. An hour later, she left Bertha Van Norman anaesthetized, resting comfortably and no longer pregnant.

"Mamma, I want you to come close," Bertha said in a barely audible tone. "I want to tell you something. Mamma, you won't make any trouble for Ray, will you?"

Beatrice shook her head.

"Mamma, I can't never get well. I will tell you, Mamma, why and the cause of my death. I can't die until I tell you."

Tears welled up at the corners of Beatrice's eyes. "What was it, Bertha?" Beatrice choked back a tear.

"I was in trouble."

"In trouble?"

"Yes," Bertha said, her voice nothing but a hoarse whisper.

"What kind of trouble? In a family way?"

"Yes, Mamma, I was." She looked away but continued to whisper. "There was an old lady operated on me. She didn't operate right on me, it was wrong, and that is the cause of my death."

"Bertha, are you sure you was in trouble?"

"Yes, Mamma, I am sure I was in trouble."

"How did you know?"

"The lady showed me my baby."

"Who was that old lady?"

"It was Mrs. Dr. Smith."

"Bertha, how far was you?"

"Three months."

Beatrice gripped her daughter's right hand and gave it a gentle squeeze. Bertha managed a slight smile. She gasped slightly, and then her eyes glazed over, her gaze fixed on a spot at the corner of the room. She was dead, and "Auntie" Smith was in big trouble.

Detective Jakeway rapped on the front door of "Auntie" Smith's house at the corner of Hall and Madison Streets. With Coroner Reuber Maurits by his side, he waited for her to answer the door.

Jakeway almost felt sorry for her. Rather than a cantankerous crone, Jennie Smith was an affable, matronly older lady. It was easy to see how young women in trouble could trust her.

But the deeper Jakeway dug, the more evidence he had uncovered implicating "Auntie" as a fairly busy midwife specializing in abortions. Old-timers spoke about a trial, twenty years earlier, in which Smith had faced and beaten a charge of performing an abortion.

"Auntie" Smith peeped from behind a half-opened door. The color drained from her cheeks when Jakeway said he wanted to talk to her. She said she suffered from failing kidneys, so Maurits summoned an ambulance.

The two men, each grasping one of the suspect's arms, helped her into the ambulance. Jakeway glanced over his shoulder to make sure Smith wasn't listening and then directed the driver to go to the county jail instead of the hospital.

Back in his office, Prosecutor William B. Brown, moved by the dying woman's declaration, planned to charge Smith with the murders of Bertha Van Norman and her unborn child.

Dr. Smith sat on the cot in her cell at the county jail. She scowled at Detective Sherman Jakeway, who stood in the corridor and listened as an *Evening Press* reporter interviewed his latest collar—a woman destined to become one of the county's most notorious inmates. Jakeway had just returned from Smith's house, which he turned upside down looking for clues.

In the twenty-four hours since the Van Norman girl died, Jakeway had unmasked the real "Dr. Smith" as sixty-seven-year-old California J.S. Smith, also known at various times by various people as "Jennie," "Mary" and "Auntie."

N. V. HENDERSON ELEVATOR AND MILLS, 88. DIVISION STREET AM

Smith James A, removed to Toledo, O.
Smith James E, ice 294 Jones, h same, **Citizens Tel 2860.**
Smith James E, gateman G R & I Ry, h 523 Butterworth
    avenue.
Smith James F, foreman G R Brush Co, rms 380 E Ful-
    ton.
Smith James H (aged 61), died July 27, 1901.
Smith James W, section hd, h 161 9th av.
Smith James W, tmstr, h 255 Travis av.
Smith Jane E (wid Aristobulos B; aged 83), died March
    24, 1902.
Smith Jay V, bd's 13 Pearl.
Smith Jennie, bds 167 Jennette.
Smith Jennie, capmkr Donker Bros, bds 431 Fremont.
Smith Mrs Jennie, physician 689 Madison av, h same.
Smith Jennie V, clk, bds 102 Barclay.
Smith Jerome H, barber F A Miner, h 12 Blumrich av.

"Mrs. Jennie Smith, physician," listed in R.L. Polk & Co.'s 1902 *Grand Rapids City Directory*. Smith offered her services as a midwife from her residence on Madison Avenue. As "Auntie" Smith, she offered other services.

She was born California Jordan in Leroy, Michigan, in 1837. At sixteen, she became "Mrs. Staring" when she married the first of her three husbands, twenty-two-year-old Edward Staring, in 1853. She became "Mrs. Wilcox" when she married Charles J. Wilcox of Battle Creek in 1870. She swapped "Wilcox" for "Smith" when she wed a Kalamazoo native. She divorced for the third and last time in 1883 and moved to Grand Rapids.

She wasn't a trained doctor, although she presented herself as a physician, offering midwife services from her home on Madison Avenue. Meanwhile, she provided another service behind closed doors. When an "inmate" of a brothel became pregnant or a young girl found herself in trouble after a premarital tryst, she called on "Dr." Smith. As a back-alley abortionist, "Auntie" was part of the city's shadow world that was peopled with characters who, during the daytime, assumed the innocent appearance of laborers and domestics but at night worked at brothels, gambling dens or unlicensed saloons.

"Dr." Smith denied even knowing Bertha, but Detective Jakeway could put her in the same building on South Division where Bertha had lived on the date of the illicit surgery. Jakeway canvassed the complex and found two residents who said they saw a woman known as "Auntie" go into Van Norman's room. Jakeway escorted the two women to Jennie

Smith's house on Madison. Jennie Smith, they swore, was the same woman whom Bertha called "Auntie."

Jakeway chuckled as Smith carped to the reporter about the way Coroner Reuber Maurits had tricked her into the jail. "He [the coroner] said he was going to take me to the hospital, and when we stopped in front of this place the man who rode in the ambulance with me said gruffly that I was going to the jail."

Smith leered at Jakeway. "I never did this horrible thing. I don't see why an old woman, sick and feeble and weak like me, should be persecuted. I don't know this girl."

The reporter asked if she had visited the residence at 232 South Division where Bertha Van Norman went under the knife.

She squinted, her eyes buried under layers of wrinkles, and glared at Jakeway for a few seconds. She was too tired, she said, to continue the interview.

After listening to the testimony of Detective Jakeway and Dr. Lee at the coroner's inquest, it took the jury just fifteen minutes to decide that Bertha Van Norman had died as a direct result of an illegal operation performed by Califernia Smith.

Coroner Reuber Maurits scribbled "septic peritonitis" as the official cause of death and "Criminal Abortion" as a "contributory factor" on the official death certificate. That night—September 27, 1902—the case became headline news. Reporters, careful to avoid the word "abortion," stated that Bertha Van Norman had died as a result of a "criminal surgery," but area residents could read between the lines.

Over the next week, the case became a fixture on page five of the *Grand Rapids Herald*, a page devoted to the city's crime-related news. The city's socialites eagerly flipped to page five and devoured the stories, their faces turning pinker with each paragraph. Older society matrons choked up at the thought of a sixteen-year-old in such trouble. They thought of their own daughters and immediately became suspicious of all gentlemen suitors. For young ladies, the story was a cautionary tale. They took silent oaths to stay chaste until after they walked down the aisle.

While Jennie Smith languished inside the Kent County Jail, Detective Sherman Jakeway joined the throng crowding into Mecosta County Courthouse to hear the testimony of Delia Willett, the key figure in a case the newspapers called "a sensation." Jakeway managed to somehow squeeze onto a bench in the gallery. The entire female population of Big Rapids, it seemed, had turned out to hear about the shocking story straight from the lips of seventeen-year-old Willett. The Big Rapids teenager had become a crucial character in Jakeway's investigation.

After depositing Smith at the jail in late September, Jakeway continued digging for clues about the enigmatic "Auntie." He wanted to find substantiation for the rumor that Smith had helped other girls "in trouble." He found what he was looking for in Big Rapids, where he uncovered a scandal bearing an uncanny resemblance to the Van Norman case when he interviewed Willett.

Jakeway identified a mirror image of Bertha Van Norman in Delia Willett, a seventeen-year-old who had had an affair with a twenty-seven-

A cabinet photograph of jurors in an 1889 murder trial that took place in Decatur, Illinois. Juries of the era consisted entirely of men. Many states did not allow female jurors until women gained the right to vote. In Michigan, women began serving on juries in 1918. *Author's collection.*

year-old teacher named Thomas H. Scott. Facing the formidable big-city detective, Willett broke down and spilled the story of a premarital affair that led to an unplanned pregnancy. When drugs failed to induce an abortion, the frightened girl said, Scott took her to visit "Auntie" Smith in Grand Rapids.

News of the affair rocked Big Rapids and prompted the local prosecutor to press charges against Scott for a single charge of using drugs in an attempt to abort Willett's pregnancy.

All eyes watched as Delia Willett gingerly tiptoed to the witness stand to begin her testimony. Thomas H. Scott nervously shifted his weight in his chair while the teenager described her love affair with Scott and how he had fed her several doses of turpentine and opium in an attempt to induce a miscarriage. When these didn't work, he took her to Grand Rapids, where "Auntie" helped her out of trouble. Wiping away tears rolling down her cheeks, Willett described the abortion in detail graphic enough to elicit gasps from the women in the gallery.

Her story also disgusted the jurors. After a short deliberation, they found Scott guilty of attempting to cause an abortion by feeding medicine to his teenage lover. For this crime, he received a year in the Detroit House of Correction.

At the conclusion of the trial later that afternoon, Jakeway boarded a train bound for Grand Rapids. When he arrived, he met with Brown and described the trial's star witness. Willett's testimony helped sway twelve men in Big Rapids. Prosecutor Brown hoped it would do the same in Grand Rapids.

The trial of California J.S. "Auntie" Smith opened to a standing-room-only crowd of mostly women on Monday, January 5, 1903. Prosecutor William Brown reduced the charge to a single count of manslaughter, punishable by up to fifteen years in prison—a daunting number for a sixty-three-year-old defendant.

Brown's case hinged on the dying declaration of Bertha Van Norman. After a legal wrangle between Brown and Smith's attorney, William D. Fuller, Judge Newnham ruled the deathbed confession admissible.

One by one, Brown called the three witnesses who had heard Bertha spill her guts about how Smith helped her with the unwanted pregnancy.

Lawyers in top hats amble about Pearl Street, circa 1870–90, in a stereograph produced by Schuyler Baldwin. The office of W.D. Fuller, who represented California J.S. Smith during her 1903 trial, is at the right. *Author's collection.*

Like participants in a séance, they raised the dead girl's voice by repeating Bertha's story. Each testified that Bertha Van Norman attributed her death to a sloppy operation performed by "Auntie" Smith.

Brown kept his most potent witness for last. He called Delia Willett to testify about her visit to "Auntie" Smith in Grand Rapids. Her voice quivering, Willett choked back tears as she explained how she traveled to Grand Rapids in August to visit "Auntie" Smith. The ladies in the gallery gasped as the witness once again described how Smith had aborted her pregnancy.

In a last-ditch effort to clear his client, Fuller put California Smith on the stand.

In an even, unbroken tone, she admitted to visiting 232 South Division, where she said she conducted an examination of Bertha Van Norman. But, she insisted, she did not perform an operation. Instead, she suggested that Bertha call a physician.

William Brown's cross-examination took nearly two hours. Under relentless questioning, Smith contradicted herself and suffered from convenient lapses of memory.

Most embarrassing was Smith's recounting, teased from the witness box by Brown, of how Detective Jakeway had caught her in a damning lie. When Smith first denied knowing Bertha Van Norman, Jakeway brought Bertha's landlady, Mrs. Lydia Beebe, to the county jail. Mrs. Beebe needed only one glance to identify California Smith as Bertha's "Auntie."

As the trial neared its climax with closing arguments, it became evident that the ordeal had taken its toll on the elderly defendant. "Mrs. Smith," observed a *Grand Rapids Herald* reporter, "is becoming visibly nervous and weakened under the strain of the trial, and yesterday, during the course of attorney's arguments, she frequently burst into tears."

"Auntie" Smith, exhausted, slowly stood as the jury shuffled back into the courtroom. She had wept the entire thirty-five-minute period it took for the twelve men to reach a decision. The jurors had listened very carefully to Bertha's deathbed confession, which Judge Newnham noted was reliable "because a person lying in the fear of imminent death is under a more potent power toward truth than can be administered by an oath in court." They also listened very carefully to the testimony of Delia Willett.

All eyes focused on the quivering figure as the foreman of the jury announced the verdict: "Guilty as charged." At that point, Smith's demeanor changed. "Then her face became hard and stern," noted the *Herald* writer, "and she showed no signs of emotion as she was led back to the jail by the court officers."

The next morning—January 10, 1903—Smith made one final appearance in court for sentencing. She faced the possible fifteen-year sentence with trepidation. An *Evening Press* reporter described the pathetic character who slowly stepped into court: "She entered the crowded court room…moaning aloud and crying for mercy."

"I am at the mercy of this court," she wailed, "and I am an innocent woman. Before God and man, I am an innocent woman."

Judge Newnham paused, waiting for Smith to settle down. "I wish I could believe you are innocent. The evidence, however, is overwhelmingly against you and convincing of your guilt."

"I know it," she whimpered and then buried her face in the folds of her dress.

"I am sorry to find that you have devoted practically your entire life to this practice of which you have been found guilty," the judge continued. "Twenty years ago you were arrested for this offense and tried, and although you were found not guilty, there must have been some basis for the prosecution. Your reputation is bad in this community and in others. There is nothing so low or so vile as that business which you made your trade and it is deserving of the severest punishment at the hands of the law. The girl upon whom you operated should have been an ornament to society, but instead she is today in her grave. Her death is at your door."

Smith continued to sob as Newnham scolded her. "It seems to me that only your gray hairs and advanced age speak for clemency in your case."

Smith wiped her eyes and stared at the judge. "Were

Califernia Smith faces the judge for sentencing in a sketch that appeared in the January 10, 1903 edition of the *Evening Post* under the headline "Seven Years in Detroit!"

it not for them," Newnham continued, "I certainly should inflict the severest penalty which the law allows. As it is, it is necessary that such a punishment be inflicted as will serve as a sufficient return for your long career of misdoing and be a warning to others. I sincerely hope this will be the last time that you will be before the bar to answer to such an offense."

Smith's knees buckled when she heard "seven years" followed by the rapping of a gavel. She held on to Fuller's arm to steady herself for a few minutes. Then she dropped into the chair, slapped her hands over her face and continued to cry.

Fuller placed his hand on her shoulder and promised he would get her sentence reduced. At her age, she could possibly die in prison, transforming Newnham's mercy sentence of seven years into life.

Califernia Smith went from Grand Rapids to the Detroit House of Correction to begin her sentence. As Fuller feared, the seven years amounted to a life sentence. After fourteen months behind bars, Califernia J.S. Smith died on March 29, 1904, of "Heart Failure" caused by "General Debility."

A guard stands watch over the Detroit House of Corrections—the only facility in turn-of-the-century Michigan to house female inmates serving long-term sentences. *Detroit Publishing Company, Library of Congress.*

SPEED DEMON

On the afternoon Califernia Smith took the stand in Superior Court—January 7, 1903—a curious case came up in police court. Frank Schermerhorn, who worked as an automobile machinist for Adams & Hart, faced a charge of violating the city's nascent automobile ordinance.

A few days earlier, Schermerhorn had zipped down Pearl Street in his "horseless carriage" at a reckless clip. An elderly man, unaccustomed to the speed of the automotive age, was crossing the street directly in Schermerhorn's path. Patrolman Clarence Boyd raced to the old man's rescue and was nearly sideswiped by the speeding motorist.

"STOP!" Boyd shouted, his voice barely audible over the machine's engine. Oblivious to the commotion he had caused, Schermerhorn continued to motor down Pearl, nearly missing a trolley along the way. The car didn't have plates (in Grand Rapids, they weren't required until September 1903), but Boyd recognized the driver.

Schermerhorn's speed landed him in police court, where he initially pleaded "not guilty" but offered to pay a minor fine to avoid the hassle of an examination. Incensed by what he perceived to be a half-baked bribe, Judge William H. Haggerty ordered a trial. Defeated, Schermerhorn changed his plea to "guilty" but moaned that it was all much ado about nothing; no automobile driver, he complained, paid any attention to the speed laws.

After listening to Clarence Boyd's narration, Haggerty fined Schermerhorn three dollars in addition to court costs for exceeding the speed limit of seven miles per hour. The next morning, a clever *Grand Rapids Herald* reporter chided Schermerhorn by nicknaming him "Automobile Scorcher."

6
"GHASTLY EXHIBIT"

The Murder Trial of
Mrs. Nancy Jeanette Flood, 1903

A shotgun at close range is a terrible weapon. The back of London's head and the top was completely blown away…his blood and portions of the skull and brains were thrown clear across the room.
—Evening Press, *April 24, 1903*

On Friday, October 30, 1903, Kent County prosecutor William B. Brown treated court-goers to a macabre, Halloween-like display.

Brown held up a pasteboard box containing a key piece of evidence in the *People v. Nancy Jeanette Flood*: the shattered skull of her alleged victim, John London. Judge Cyrus E. Perkins had, at Brown's request, ordered the exhumation of London's body for the purpose of bringing the skull into court. The broken skull, Perkins reasoned, would provide the jury with the most graphic way to visualize John London's wounds—suffered six months earlier, on April 21, 1903.

The courtroom gallery fell silent as Brown lifted the lid and reached into the box.

A chorus of "oohs" and "ahs" erupted from the gallery as Brown pulled John London's skull from the box. Cradling it in his palms, he held it in the air so Judge Perkins and the members of the jury could see it before handing it to defense attorney C.G. Turner.

Mrs. Flood leaned forward and studied the skull with curiosity. Although she appeared emotionless, the pace with which she masticated her gum increased, hinting at a degree of nervousness underneath the cool façade.

Turner handed the skull back to Brown, who passed it to the witness, Coroner Hilliker. The entire exchange resembled a grotesque version of "hot potato."

Hilliker balanced the skull in his left palm while he demonstrated the effects of a shotgun blast at point-blank range with his right hand. The initial blast of fifty pellets, he explained, entered London's skull in the back. He jabbed his index finger through the hole in the back of the skull. The cluster exited the skull above the right ear, blowing a large hole in the right parietal bone. Hilliker thrust his index and forefingers into the chasm and quickly pulled them out, mimicking the movement of the shot that obliterated John London's brain.

A burst of gas, he explained, followed the pellets into the skull and erupted like a stick of dynamite in a clay pot, blowing the top off of the cranium. He cupped his fingers and dipped them into the gaping hole in the skull cap, making a scooping motion. The force of the blast ripped the scalp from right ear to left eye and fractured the remaining portions of the skull, giving it a spider web–like appearance.

Forty-year-old Nancy Jeanette Flood listened intently as Hilliker testified to his belief that the gunshot was fired into the back of London's head and that, given the circumstances, it would have been impossible for him to have either shot himself or have died when his gun misfired. This—that the entrance wound was not in the front but in the back of London's head—was the crux of the people's case.

Several times, Mrs. Flood leaned toward her attorney and whispered, her every move watched with fascination. Despite the gruesome display taking place on the witness stand, Mrs. Flood captivated the attention of morbid curiosity-seekers, who crowded into the courthouse to witness the real-life drama of a murder trial. The onlookers, including representatives of the local papers, found Mrs. Flood's demeanor as interesting as the ghoulish exhibits. For a week, she had followed the proceedings with stolid indifference that many observers found unfathomable for a woman facing a life sentence for murder.

"She pulled to pieces the little sprig of evergreen which she brought into the court room with her in the morning," observed a curious *Evening Press* correspondent at the onset of the trial, "and chewed incessantly on the gum, which has been her solace ever since the trial began."

Widow Flood had immigrated to Michigan from Canada twenty-five years earlier, in 1878. She settled in Grand Rapids, where she met James Flood. They had two children together before Flood died in 1883 amid rumors of

Jennie Flood kept her head bowed for much of her murder trial, as shown in this sketch drawn by an *Evening Press* artist.

foul play. Neighbors didn't fail to notice that the Flood farm on the outskirts of the city was heavily indebted and that, shortly after his death, the widow collected $2,500 from his life insurance.

She looked much younger than forty and had a matronly appearance that was totally incongruous with the image of a wicked witch who allegedly perpetrated, in the words of a *Grand Rapids Herald* reporter, "one of the most remarkable insurance and murder plots in the history of the state."

One by one, witnesses took the stand and described events that had unfolded six months earlier on the farm of Barney Fingleton.

The sun hovered above the tree line on April 21, 1903, as Undersheriff John Verkerke led a group to the porch of the Fingleton farm in Cannon Township, a few miles east of town. They were responding to a report that forty-four-year-old farmhand John London had sustained a fatal gunshot wound to the head when his double-barrel shotgun accidentally misfired.

This sketch of the Fingleton farmhouse, drawn by an *Evening Press* artist, appeared in the April 25, 1903 edition.

London, a sort of handyman and farmhand wrapped into one, lived on the farm with sixty-eight-year-old Barney Fingleton. Both men enjoyed the financial support of Nancy Jeanette Flood, who had purchased Fingleton's farm a few months earlier with the understanding that the old man would live out the rest of his days in the farmhouse. It was a peculiar arrangement that caused the gossips to spread venomous rumors about a covert love affair between Flood and London and about a possible love triangle with the comely widow positioned between London and old man Fingleton.

Deputy Pettis, who knew all three, spotted Fingleton on the porch.

"What have you got here, Barney?" Pettis said.

"Ed, it's awful." Fingleton opened the door, and Pettis brushed past him into the farmhouse. After a few seconds, he emerged, his face ashen. He wiped spittle from his mouth and gestured for the others to come inside.

In all his years as county coroner, Dr. Simeon Le Roy had never seen a more ghastly sight.

London's body lay on the floor under a white sheet mottled with crimson patches. The wall in front of his chair and the ceiling above where he sat were speckled with dots of blood and flecks of brain tissue. About five feet away from the body was a small pool of blood with a heap of gray brain tissue at its center. Along the west wall sat a potbelly stove, spattered with blood and minute bits of brain matter.

Le Roy pulled the sheet back to examine the body. Most of the calvarium and right parietal portions of the skull were missing. The force of the blast shredded London's scalp; a large, skin flap covered his face. Le Roy gently lifted the bloody veil to reveal what was left of the victim's face. John London stared at him with one lifeless eye, the other blown from its socket and dangling from the optic nerve like a ball on a tether.

As the officers examined the scene, Fingleton explained what had happened. They were in the barn hitching Flood's horse when they heard a gunshot emanate from the vicinity of the kitchen. At first, Fingleton thought that London had shot the neighbor's dog. The day before, the dog attacked London's pet ferret, and just that morning, London had sworn he would even the score.

Jennie Flood picked up the narration.

"Fingleton said at once: 'John has shot McCormick's dog,' but remembering that I had cautioned the McCormick boy to keep the dog tied up when the animal injured London's ferret, I laughed at the idea and continued to the house. When I opened the door, I gasped involuntarily, and Fingleton without a word passed ahead. London half lay and half sat in his chair at the table. The muscles were relaxing and the body was slowly slipping out of the chair when I told Fingleton to lay him on the floor." Fingleton then pulled London's body from the chair and covered it with a white sheet.

Flood explained that London kept his shotgun in the pantry, and he always kept it loaded. She pointed to the room just a few feet away from the chair.

Deputy Pettis eyed the shotgun lying in the doorjamb of the pantry. He stood on the chair and looked at the ceiling. The plaster was splattered by blood, particles of skin from London's scalp and brain matter. Pettis also thought that he saw hairs pasted to the ceiling by coagulating blood. A series of pockmarks indicated that the blast may have come from directly below. "Suicide," he whispered.

"I don't think so," Flood said. "I don't think John would commit suicide. He was happy."

Le Roy interrupted. Some of the pellets could have deflected off of London's skull and landed in the ceiling. The pattern of wounds suggested that the shot entered the back right side of London's head.

"That gun of London's went off accidentally," Fingleton interrupted. "One of the locks was worn and sometimes failed to catch when the hammer was brought to full cock."

Mrs. Flood agreed. Pettis shrugged and sat in the chair as he listened to her explain how London might have died when his shotgun accidentally discharged.

A sketch of the London crime scene drawn by an *Evening Press* artist.

London, she said, kept his shotgun in the pantry, and he always left it sitting with both hammers cocked. Sitting in the chair, he must have reached for the weapon when it caught the doorframe and discharged. The weapon, Flood explained, had a loose trigger, which caused it to accidentally fire. She and London often went hunting in the woods around the Fingleton farm, and she had witnessed just such an accident.

Pettis picked up the shotgun, set it upright against the inside wall of the pantry and glanced at Flood, who nodded. That was where London kept the gun.

Pettis sat down at the kitchen table and threw his arm back, but he couldn't reach the gun.

That evening, under the dim electric lighting of O'Brien Bros. undertaking establishment, Dr. Le Roy examined John London. After studying the head wounds, he concluded that the deadly shot came from a horizontal, not vertical, position and from the back left side. The injuries seemed to corroborate Mrs. Flood's belief that John London's gun had accidentally discharged while he pulled it from the pantry. Still, there was something fishy

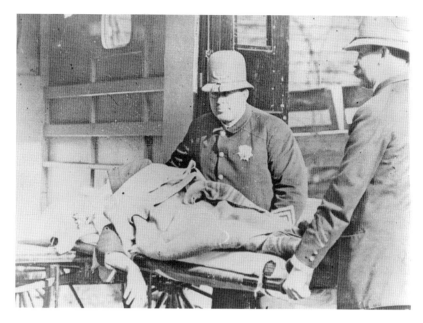

Constables load a body into a horse-drawn wagon in this photograph, circa 1900.
Grand Rapids History & Special Collections, Archives, Grand Rapids Public Library.

about the entry wound in the back of London's skull. The shoe-shaped hole indicated that London was facing the other direction—toward the kitchen table—while reaching for the weapon.

Le Roy stood erect and threw his arm backward as if reaching for something. He felt his deltoid muscles stretch as he grasped at the air. It was a difficult, if not impossible, position from which to clutch a weapon weighing in excess of ten pounds.

Besides, a tight contact—the edge of the gun barrel pressed against the scalp—would have been necessary for the explosion that blew fragments of London's skull into the air. If the barrel wasn't held against London's head, the gas would not have detonated inside the cranium. And an accidental discharge made a tight-contact wound hard to imagine.

Dr. Le Roy pried open London's jaws and stared, in astonishment, at a mouthful of partially chewed chicken. It was possible that London had taken a bite just before reaching for his gun, but it didn't seem very likely.

He now suspected that someone shot John London from a spot inside the pantry. If his suspicions proved correct, then two suspects emerged: Barney Fingleton and Jennie Flood.

Dr. Le Roy turned to the telephone.

After discussing matters with Kent County sheriff Leman Chapman, Dr. Le Roy and Deputy Charles Gates made a second trip to the farmhouse to examine the pockmarked ceiling.

Le Roy stood on the chair and examined the indentations in the plaster above where London had eaten his last meal. If the shot came from directly below, the pellets would have struck the ceiling first, followed by the blood spray. Yet it appeared that several of the pocks ran through the blood, as if they were made afterward. It didn't make sense.

Then Gates spied a metal file on the stove and handed it to Le Roy, who gently inserted it into one of the gouges. It fit perfectly. Someone, using the file, had repeatedly gouged the ceiling in order to make it look like the gun went off while in a vertical position.

Gates stared at the chair as he envisioned John London's final moments. After Jennie Flood served his lunch, London sat down at the table and began eating. He didn't suspect a thing or perhaps didn't even notice as Mrs. Flood tiptoed into the pantry behind him.

Gates moved into the pantry. Flood would have positioned herself behind the doorframe to prevent any blood from hitting her dress. She gently raised the barrel of London's shotgun and inched it forward until it touched the back of London's scalp. She squeezed the trigger before he could react to the feeling of cold steel. After the shot, London slumped to the side, the right side of his head striking the floorboards and leaving a puddle of blood and brain matter.

Undaunted, Jennie Flood then quickly grabbed the file, stood on the chair and began jabbing holes in the ceiling.

Gates realized that they faced a cold-hearted killer who wouldn't flinch at doctoring the bloody spectacle to fit her needs, but she had committed a critical error in judgment by not moving the chair closer to the pantry. John London could not have reached the gun from that distance or from that angle.

"What work was done to cover up the crime was well done," he later remarked to a reporter, "but the murderess skipped some important details that are leaking out and overdid herself in establishing the characteristics of an accident."

Sheriff Leman Chapman strutted into Prosecutor William Brown's office with a sheaf of papers under his arm: evidence, he believed, in a plot to murder John London and collect on a life insurance policy.

Chapman's detectives interviewed Norman W. Mather, an insurance agent. According to Mather, Jennie Flood had purchased—ostensibly at John London's request—three different policies. According to Mather, she also tried to purchase a fourth policy in the staggering sum of $20,000. The massive amount, however, triggered suspicions, and Aetna refused to underwrite London.

Chapman placed a series of handwritten papers across Brown's desk: the applications for three life insurance policies taken out in London's name. Next to the applications, Chapman placed known samples of Jennie Flood's and John London's handwriting.

Brown leaned closer to the papers and inspected the writing on the insurance applications, comparing them to a letter inked by John London. Anyone would conclude that the penmanship didn't match. Besides, London's letter contained numerous spelling errors in basic words such as "have" and "write," whereas relatively complicated words such as "benefactress" were spelled correctly on the applications.

Next, he compared the signatures on the applications with known signatures of both Flood and Fingleton. Placing them side by side, it became evident that Jennie Flood had filled out the insurance applications. It was possible that she scripted them with London's full knowledge and cooperation, but they also presented a powerful motive for murder; in the event of London's death, his "benefactress"—Jennie Flood—would receive the settlement. This is why,

Vital evidence in the prosecution's case against Jennie Flood included signatures on John London's insurance applications. In presenting the case to the reading public, the *Evening Press* printed facsimiles of these signatures. This one, taken from a life insurance application in London's name, was allegedly written by Jennie Flood.

Brown realized, Jennie Flood had insisted that London's gun misfired. An insurance company would not pay in the event of suicide.

And, it appeared, both Jennie Flood and Barney Fingleton would need the money in the near future. Fingleton had recently sold his farm to Flood, and as part of the deal, she agreed to care for him for the rest of his life. Probate court records revealed Fingleton's ulterior motive; he had sold the farm amid accusations of mishandling his niece's finances. The probate court was about to rule against him, and it appeared he sold the farm to avoid losing it in the court proceedings. This subterfuge was about to cost the Widow Flood, who owed money on Fingleton's property as well as on her own farm. Costly reparation could lead her to bankruptcy court unless she all of a sudden came into a hefty sum of cash.

The evidence painted a convincing portrait of Fingleton as a willing accomplice to murder, although detectives found something that suggested a different scenario. Mrs. Flood had apparently attempted to take out a life insurance policy on Barney Fingleton, too.

One way or the other, Fingleton knew something. Brown ordered the immediate arrest of Flood on a charge of murder in the first degree and Fingleton on a charge of accessory to murder.

While Brown prepared to convene a grand jury, Jennie Flood sat with an *Evening Press* reporter and gave a lengthy statement:

> *I have known John London more than twenty years. He never had any money to speak of and was on the verge of becoming a county charge on more than one occasion. I have befriended him more than once and was his confidant in many ways. I know he did not commit suicide. He was not that kind of a man; had not the nerve, so to speak. I believe his death was purely accidental.*

She paused as the reporter scribbled in his notebook.

The reporter, who had heard rumors about the investigation underway and whispers about a love triangle, then asked the question hounding detectives working the case: "Do you know of anyone who might have a motive for killing London? Had not he had trouble with Fingleton because the latter was jealous of London's intimacy with you?"

Mrs. Flood repositioned herself in the chair and smiled. "Oh, no," she said. "John felt Fingleton to be his best friend. Fingleton was not jealous. There was no reason for it. In the first place he had no right to be, and one look would convince most any person that John London was not the person to create jealousy."

"Do you know if John London carried life insurance?"

Flood's smile evaporated. She cleared her throat before responding. "I do not. He had often mentioned that life insurance should be carried by every man of family, but he never had any that I knew of."

When Jennie Flood returned to her farm on the afternoon of April 23, 1903, Deputy Gates was waiting on the front porch with a pair of handcuffs dangling in his grip.

With Flood safely behind bars in the Kent County Jail, Deputy Gates traveled to Fingleton's farm on Friday, April 24, 1903.

Fingleton stood on the front porch and watched as Gates stepped toward the farmhouse.

"Are they going to lock me up?" he whined.

"I guess they are, Barney. They don't think you have told all you know."

Gates clamped a pair of bracelets over Fingleton's wrists and helped him into the carriage. As they made their way toward the jail, Gates noted that Fingleton would face an accessory charge if he didn't come clean about London's death.

On the ride back to town, Fingleton spilled his guts. He went back on his earlier statement and now said that when he heard the shot coming from the farmhouse, he turned to see Jennie Flood emerging from the kitchen with her hands clasped to her stomach. At first, he thought she had been shot.

"Are you shot?" He yelled.

"No, it's John," she said without a hint of emotion in her voice.

Fingleton's eyes widened when Gates told him about Flood's attempts to purchase a life insurance policy in his name. He then realized that he may have narrowly escaped John London's fate.

As soon as Fingleton inked his signature to the affidavit, Leman H. Chapman plucked it from his fingers and took it to Flood's cell with the hope of prying a confession out of his stubborn prisoner.

"It looks to me as if you were up against the real thing, and it would be best for you to make a clean breast of it," he said.

He explained that Fingleton had a change of heart. The old man whimpered like a little girl as he changed his story. Chapman summarized the affidavit he held in his hand.

Jennie Flood smirked. "Did he say that?"

"Yes, and I have his affidavit to it." Chapman waved the paper in front of Flood, who sat on the cell cot, unmoved by the chief's theatrics.

"Well, if I am convicted, it will be circumstantial evidence that will do it."

Chapman reminded Flood that Fingleton's new statement placed her inside the farmhouse during the shooting. "You talk about circumstantial evidence, how are you going to get around that?"

"Did Barney say that?"

"Yes, and I have his affidavit." Again, Chapman held up the paper.

"Would it hurt my case?"

Chapman nodded.

"Well, I won't talk any more till I get counsel."

Livery barns in the area of the courthouse filled up on Monday, April 27, 1903, as people traveled from near and far to watch the preliminary hearing of Jennie Flood.

An *Evening Press* reporter described the now-infamous widow's demeanor as she waltzed into the Farmers' Club Room: "Mrs. Flood seemed in no way changed when she was brought from the jail by the deputy. She had the same firm expression which is peculiar to her and really did not seem at all nervous over the terrible charge which is hanging over her."

Jennie Flood took the stand first and began a line of testimony that lasted an hour. Grilled by Prosecutor William Brown, she repeated her story of hearing the gunshot and racing into the kitchen to find the bloody spectacle of John London slumped down in his chair.

Brown smirked and shook his head. "As a matter of fact, had you not returned to the house before the shot was fired and left Barney there?"

The majestic courthouse of Grand Rapids, circa 1900–10. *Detroit Publishing Company, Library of Congress.*

"Certainly not," Flood said in a monotone voice. "How could I when we were both at the barn?"

Brown stared at Flood for a few seconds before proceeding. His next line of questions was vital to proving Flood's motive. "Was Fingleton ever insured with a policy running to you?"

"I don't know. He did once, but I don't think it was kept up. You see, he was to insure me and I him."

"Did you take out the insurance for him or did he look after it himself?"

"He had as much to do with it as I."

"Did you pay the premiums or did he?"

"He did, I guess. I didn't."

"Then you know of no insurance running to you on the life of Fingleton?"

"No."

Brown paused for a few seconds before asking his next question. "Did you know of John London having his life insured?"

"He often wanted to, but I don't think he did. We had talked of it and had looked over advertisements at the Fingleton house. This was after Fingleton's old policy was taken out in the equitable."

"Did he ever get a policy?"

"Not that I know of. I never saw a policy, but I believe he did take out a sick or accident policy from a Mr. Mercer in Grand Rapids."

"Did you ever fill out an application or talk with an insurance agent with regard to London's insurance?"

"No."

This last answer sealed Jennie Flood's fate. Brown presented the insurance applications and handwriting samples to the jury and then followed that with Fingleton, who testified to seeing Flood retreating from the kitchen after the gunshot.

"She was in the house," Fingleton testified. To Brown's dismay, the witness kept talking. "She wasn't there long, and I don't believe she killed London, but she was there. That gun of London's went off accidentally. One of the locks was worn and sometimes failed to catch when the hammer was brought to full cock."

Despite Fingleton's editorial, the jury voted to indict, sending Jennie Flood to trial on a charge of murder in the first degree.

Jennie Flood, stung by Fingleton's testimony, carped all the way back to the jail.

Once inside, she spotted Fingleton about the corridors on the second floor. "I can't see where the justice in this thing is," she grumbled. "They keep me locked up tight and don't allow me even to see a paper, and Fingleton, who is every bit as guilty as I, so far as this case is concerned, is allowed the freedom of the building. I don't like it. They are discriminating against me."

Deputy Gates needed a break from all the complaining, so he remained at the base of the staircase while Jennie Flood waddled up toward her cell. He was just about to follow her up when Flood bumped into Fingleton. After an awkward silence, they began whispering something. Gates couldn't make out the dialogue, so he ascended a few steps. He caught the incriminating tail end of their chat.

"Why did you tell that?" Flood demanded, the sharpness of her tone evident despite her attempts to keep quiet.

"S—h. I had to, to get out," Fingleton responded.

The first week of testimony in the Flood trial came to an end on Saturday, October 31, with a surprise ruling from Judge Perkins. He had decided to acquiesce to Brown's request and allow the jury to visit the crime scene.

A caravan of carriages reached the Fingleton farm at midmorning. Brown, Turner and Judge Perkins each rode in separate buggies, followed by a four-horse carriage containing the jurors. Jennie Flood, accompanied by a sheriff deputy, had arrived a half hour before the others. Flood, attired in a black dress, waited on the front lawn. She enjoyed the morning sunshine—it was a welcome respite from months of confinement in the Kent County Jail.

The twelve jurors shuffled into the kitchen followed by Flood, her attorney, Brown and Judge Perkins. The sixteen bodies packed into the confined space created a nauseating sensation of claustrophobia. The jurors whispered to one another in hushed voices, as if afraid to denigrate the sanctity of the place, while they surveyed the scene. Jennie Flood watched, her hands folded, from the corner of the room.

Back in Grand Rapids, Dr. William Fuller—a professor of surgery and surgical anatomy at the Grand Rapids Medical College—conducted a chilling experiment on behalf of Flood's defense.

Dr. Fuller had just raised the shotgun when he realized that the cadaver had slumped down in the chair. He set the gun down and wrapped his arms around the cadaver's chest and tugged upward until the corpse was upright.

Once again, he raised the gun, holding it approximately half an inch from the cadaver's left temple. He squinted as he squeezed the trigger. Despite the tent of white sheets surrounding the chair, the bang of the gun's report echoed throughout the laboratory.

Setting the gun aside, Dr. Fuller leaned down and studied the wounds.

The second week of the trial opened on Monday, November 2, when Turner began his defense. His case followed a line that London had died when his shotgun accidentally misfired and thus hinged on his ability to prove that the entrance wound was in the front of London's head. To prove his point, he enlisted the help of Drs. William Fuller and Frank Lee.

In front of a standing-room-only crowd, Dr. Fuller took the stand and described the results of his experiment. The damage done to the cadaver's head was nearly identical to the wounds sustained by John London. This left one logical conclusion: the fatal shot entered through London's left temple and exited above his right ear—a position consistent with a scenario in which he was facing the pantry when the gun went off.

Just when jurors thought the trial couldn't get any bloodier, on the second day of his case, Turner entered into evidence a piece of John London's scalp recovered during the exhumation at Oak Hill Cemetery.

As soon as Turner produced the grisly relic, Brown leaped from his seat to object. Without an unbroken chain of provenance, he argued, there was no way to prove that the dried piece of skin had come from John London's head.

Turner was about to ask the prosecutor what head he thought the scalp came from when Judge Perkins interceded. He ruled the scalp admissible and asked Turner to proceed.

Turner handed the scalp to his witness, Dr. Lee. He hoped that the dried slice of skin, which looked like a piece of beef jerky with hair, would support Lee's theory that the shot had entered London's head from the front.

Lee, who had orchestrated the exhumation of London's body, had found the piece of skin tucked into the shoe-shaped hole in the back of London's skull. After briefly studying the specimen, Lee concluded the piece of scalp was likely sucked into the hole by the explosion inside London's cranium.

The *Evening Press* correspondent watched Jennie Flood's reaction to see if the scalp, which he described as "little more grewsome [*sic*] than the wigs which may be seen before any hairdresser's establishment," moved the typically stoic defendant. "She had often whispered to her attorneys during the taking of testimony, and then laughed at something amusing. But when London's scalp was exhibited in court yesterday afternoon her manner changed and she showed signs of disgust that were almost too lively considering the interest with which she had surveyed his skull earlier in the proceedings."

Brown wanted to impeach Dr. Lee by coaxing him into admitting that the flap of skin was pushed into the shoe-shaped hole when the cluster of shot entered the back of London's head. So he handed Dr. Lee the fragmented skull—which resembled a shattered eggshell held together with wires—in an attempt to determine what part of the head the piece of scalp originally covered. Dr. Lee turned over the piece in his hands before placing it on top of the reconstructed skull, but the desiccated skin had shrunk and didn't quite fit.

After a lengthy exchange about the shrinking of skin, Brown excused the witness without shaking his belief that the shot struck John London from the front.

In his closing argument, Brown addressed the key bone of contention in the trial: the position of John London when the "fatal shot" occurred:

> *Even should it be true that the fatal shot entered John London's head at a point above the left temple, as the defense has claimed, it would have been impossible for him to have shot himself accidentally in this manner. The defense has claimed that he was bending far over at the time he was shot, that the gun was accidentally discharged while he was drawing it through the pantry door and that the shot took effect as I have stated. The fact that the defense claims the shot entered above the temple is an irrefutable argument that London was not shot accidentally.*

Brown went on to describe Jennie Flood's motive for murder. "Mrs. Flood, the defendant in this case, was the only person who would benefit by London's death. It has been proved that she handed in the application and received the policy for London."

The prosecutor paused for effect. "However," he shook his index finger in the air, "she has denied anything about London having been insured."

Jennie Flood had inexplicably committed the fatal faux pas in denying her role in writing out the insurance documents—a fact Brown underscored when he placed the handwriting samples in front of the jury.

After deliberating for twenty-four hours, the jury returned its verdict on November 12, 1903. Foreman William J. Russell stood, straightened his jacket and pronounced the defendant guilty of murder in the first degree. The verdict made Jennie Flood only the second woman in Kent County, after convicted arsonist Esther Coffee in 1877, to receive a life sentence.

Jennie Flood kept her composure to the end. A *Grand Rapids Herald* reporter, impressed with the mien of the now-convicted murderess, described the scene: "When Foreman William J. Russell arose and announced the finding of the jury Mrs. Flood gave no outward evidence of the crushing blow. The same stoical indifference that has characterized her since her arrest was still maintained."

Back at the county lockup, Flood asked to see Barney Fingleton. Once again, Deputy Gates eavesdropped on the conversation.

"Well, Barney, we're done for."

"Don't talk so loud," Fingleton hissed.

"We have not the ghost of a show, Barney. They have found me guilty, and it is all off with us."

After the brief conversation, Gates escorted Flood back to her cell, where she threw herself down on the cot and pulled the bedspread over her head.

Later that night, a reporter for the *Grand Rapids Herald* visited Jennie Flood at the jail. She grasped a Bible and held it tightly against her chest. "As there is a God above," she exclaimed, "I am innocent of killing John London. I was not in the house at the time and do not know how he met death. I have always supposed that he accidentally shot himself."

She wiped her eyes with the back of her sleeve.

"There is more to this affair than has been brought out, and you can be certain of that. Someone knows something that he is not telling. I feel that I have been wrongfully treated. The case has gone against me, and I don't know why it has done so. I am as innocent of killing John London as I am of killing myself."

Name		Sex	Color	Age	Marital				Birthplace
Quimby	Sarah	Inmate	F	W	40	Wd			Michigan
Tillman	Neva	Inmate	F	W	21	M	0			Michigan
Sehlukebir	Pearl	Inmate	F	W	24	S				Michigan
Williams	Buelah	Inmate	F	W	21	M	6	1	1	Ohio
Fleming	Madge	Inmate	F	W	21	S				Kentucky
Pope	Nellie	Inmate	F	W	50	Wd		1	1	Canada
Paull	Lida	Inmate	F	W	35	M	2	1	1	Michigan
Flood	Jennie	Inmate	F	W	47	Wd		2	2	Canada
Larsen	Mabel	Inmate	F	W	34	M	14	3	3	Denmark
Jones	Lillian	Inmate	F	B	27	S				Illinois
Kerfuit	Ida	Inmate	F	Mu	28	M	8	0	0	Tennessee
McCoy	Mamie	Inmate	F	W	38	M	7	3	3	Iowa
King	Emma	Inmate	F	W	34	M	10	0	0	Michigan
Rehda	Dona	Inmate	F	W	39	D				Ireland
Cummings	Louise	Inmate	F	W	25	M	7	1	1	Michigan
Johnson	Rachel	Inmate	F	B	56	M	4	1	1	Canada
Smith	Maud	Inmate	F	Mu	33	M	3	2	2	Michigan
Reynolds	Eliza	Inmate	F	Mu	39	D				Indiana
Lewis	Elma	Inmate	F	W	19	M	2	0	0	Michigan
Russell	Gertrude	Inmate	F	W	46	Wd		2	2	Indiana
Woods	Frances	Inmate	F	W	3?		15	3	3	Michigan
McKnight	Mary	Inmate	F	W	55	Wd		2	2	Canada

This page from the 1910 census lists Jennie Flood and a few of her jail mates at the Detroit House of Corrections, including noted serial poisoner Mary McKnight. *National Archives.*

Jennie Flood had served just over a year of her life sentence in the Detroit House of Correction when Bernard Fingleton faced a jury in January 1904. The case didn't attract nearly the same fanfare. Residents of Grand Rapids, their bloodlust sated by the gruesome exhibits of the Flood trial, had grown tired of the drama, making Fingleton's day in court anticlimactic. Newspaper reporters who had devoted several columns of ink per day to the Flood trial gave a mere paragraph or two to the Fingleton case.

The same lineup of characters made a return trip to the witness stand to rehash what by now had become old news. Sheriff Chapman, whose testimony was delayed until he recovered from injuries sustained while slipping on a patch of ice, took the stand on the last day of the prosecution's case.

Chapman's testimony raised a few eyebrows. After rehashing Fingleton's first two stories about April 21, 1903, he described a third that he wasn't permitted to talk about during Jennie Flood's trial. This third story occurred during a conversation under an apple tree in Fingleton's orchard.

After Chapman showed Fingleton the insurance application Flood had taken out on London's life, the old man cracked.

Under oath, Chapman relayed Fingleton's response. "My God, is that so?" Fingleton had said, horrified as he realized Flood's apparent motive for murder. "I'll tell you the truth, the whole truth, if it is the last thing I ever say. Mrs. Flood was in the house at the time the gun went off. I had gone a few steps from the barn when I saw her enter the kitchen door and had gotten to where the trucks stand when I heard the report of the gun. I remember this because it made me nervous, and I put my hand on them to steady myself. Almost immediately Mrs. Flood appeared at the door. She held her hand across her stomach, and I called out, 'Are you hurt?' She said, 'No, it's John.' She turned back with me, and I entered the door first."

Chapman's testimony was vital corroboration of Fingleton's story, and it went a long way to creating reasonable doubt. Barney now appeared more like a dupe than a willing accomplice in Flood's murder-for-profit scheme.

On the final day of the trial, Fingleton testified in his own defense. An *Evening Press* correspondent described the withered defendant:

> *At the close of the first day that he himself spent on the witness stand he had apparently aged ten years. His slight figure seemed even slighter than before and more bowed. He no longer laughed or smiled, and the loose, wrinkled skin of his face took on a yellowish tinge in place of its former prison pallor. When finally permitted to resume his place between his attorneys, he sat with his head leaning on his hand for hours at a time.*

Prosecutor Brown grilled the defendant, who nervously tapped his fingers against the side of the witness box.

"How did London meet his death?"

"He got shot."

"Did you know of any purpose to get rid of him?"

"I did not," Fingleton said in the bold, indignant tone of a falsely accused man.

"Did you think afterward that he met his death in any other way than accidentally?"

"I did not." He scratched his cheek, which had the color and texture of antique parchment.

"Was it the belief which caused you to speak carelessly about where you were?" Brown asked, referring to the three different versions of the "truth" Fingleton told.

"It was."

Major E.C. Watkins, Fingleton's defense attorney, tried to capitalize on his client's frail condition. During closing arguments, Watkins used a powerful emotional appeal by asking jurors if they would send an ailing man to prison for the few days that remained in his life. A few jurors shielded their eyes as if embarrassed at the possibility, and several women in the gallery wept.

On January 23, 1904, the jury decided on a verdict. On his way into the courtroom, Barney Fingleton stopped to shake hands with his neighbors, who crammed into the courtroom to show their support. He appeared confident of an acquittal, but when foreman A.N. Green rose to announce the jury's verdict, Fingleton grew weak in the knees and propped himself against Major Watkins.

The gallery erupted in cheers as Green announced, "Not guilty." After months in the county jail, Barney Fingleton was a free man, and the ghastly story of John London's murder came to an end at last.

Major Watkins had underestimated his client's life expectancy by over two decades. Barney Fingleton lived in Kent County for another twenty-six years. While a resident at a house for the aged and destitute run by the Little Sisters of the Poor, he suffered a fatal stroke on March 28, 1930, at the age of ninety-five.

THE THIRTEENTH JUROR

Rodney Sessions watched the drama of the Flood trial unfold from his usual seat next to the jury box. Seventy-nine-year-old Sessions had become such a fixture at trials in Grand Rapids that reporters affectionately dubbed him the "thirteenth juror."

With the interest of a real juror, Sessions would sit, legs crossed, and tug on his right ear lobe so he could more clearly hear the testimony. He had sat next

Rodney Sessions, the "thirteenth juror," listens intently to testimony during the murder trial of Jennie Flood. This sketch appeared in the *Evening Press* of November 7, 1903.

to the jury that sent Charles Macard to Jackson for the murder of Mrs. McKendrick and many other key trials in Kent County history.

Born in Vermont in 1824, Sessions was eighty-one when the jury acquitted Barney Fingleton—the last noteworthy trial he would attend. Kent County's famous "thirteenth juror" died on December 13, 1905.

7

IN THE BAG, 1907

Then came their fatal misstep from the paths of virtue, the consequent trip to Grand Rapids to cover the evidence of their transgression, and the ensuing double tragedy.
—Grand Rapids Herald, *December 13, 1907*

Lena Williams lifted the hem of her dress and tiptoed to the edge of the Grand River. A deep freeze overnight had left the area glazed with ice on the morning of Wednesday, December 11, 1907, and she decided to forage for sticks to use as kindling in her fireplace. The frigid air had descended on the warmer river water, leaving the entire area blanketed with a thick, gauze-like mist.

Lena carried a bundle of twigs in the crook of her arm as she made her way through the wisps of fog south along the riverbank. She had collected an armful of driftwood but decided to go a little farther. Lena enjoyed the quiet solitude at the water's edge before the rest of the city awoke.

She had walked as far south as the Wagemaker Furniture Plant when she spotted a bunch of dried sticks on the shore by the Prescott Street sewer drain. As she reached down to gather them, she noticed something bobbing a few feet from shore. With a forked branch, she managed to pull the bundle to the water's edge. It was a small, leather valise that had become saturated with river water. The top of the bag was frozen shut, but after a few minutes of prying, she managed to peel back the flaps.

Her screams echoed over the water.

The fog had lifted by midmorning as Coroner Le Roy began the postmortem at the Birdsall undertaking establishment on Pearl Street.

Under the yellow glow of the incandescent lights, Le Roy opened the valise and gently pulled from it the remains of an infant—a female of about six weeks. Several hours had passed since Lena Williams discovered the baby curled inside the bag. Submerged in the icy Grand River for

Hustle and bustle in front of the E.S. Pierce clothing store at the corner of Monroe and Pearl Streets, from a Schuyler Baldwin stereograph, circa 1870–90. *Author's collection.*

several hours, the frosted corpse had thawed just enough for the coroner to begin his examination.

He gently set the baby on the table and handed the valise to Detective Warren W. Sturgis, a veteran detective tapped by Superintendent Carr to solve the macabre mystery posed by the baby in the bag.

Sturgis cast a glance at the baby. Her eyes were open and her pupils fixed, as if she were staring at some spot in the distance. Her upper lip, with an adorable cupid's bow, had turned a cyanotic hue, and her lips were parted as if she was about to coo.

He sharply turned away. It was a difficult sight for the thirty-nine-year-old cop.

He and his wife, Gerda, had tried to begin a family, and when Gerda finally became pregnant in 1903, she suffered a miscarriage. A few weeks later, on January 6, 1904, she died of acute albuminuria.

Sturgis took a deep breath and turned his attention to the valise. Perhaps somewhere inside the bag he would find a clue to the identity of the depraved person responsible for drowning the infant.

The valise had been pierced on all four sides, with two gaping holes cut into the top just above where the baby's face had been—likely air holes, which indicated that the infant was alive when she entered the water. Another hole was evidently made to remove an identifying mark.

The bag contained several items of baby clothing. Sturgis removed them one by one and laid them out on a table. The mini-trousseau contained blankets, dresses and shirts trimmed with pink lace. None of the pink-fringed garments contained any identifying remarks, but the high quality of the material suggested that the baby's parents were far from destitute.

Behind him, he heard Le Roy's voice: "Infant female, approximately six weeks old…"

Sturgis hummed a tune to drown out the snipping sounds coming from the mortuary table as Le Roy began cutting. Next to the handle of the satchel was a rough patch where someone had scratched away the leather to obliterate an identifying mark of some sort. There was another spot of scratched leather just inside the lip of the valise, but this time the blue pencil inscription remained just barely legible.

Sturgis leaned forward and examined the markings: "Ed Titus, Cloverdale, Barry County." He jotted the name onto a piece of paper.

Within the hour, Le Roy had finished his postmortem and briefed Sturgis about his findings. He found no external signs of violence and no evidence of disease. The baby had died either from exposure or drowning. This led to one logical conclusion: she had been murdered.

Sturgis knew where to start. He glanced at the paper in his hand.

By noon, Sturgis had identified "Ed Titus" as a forty-year-old, well-respected resident of Cloverdale.

Sturgis phoned Titus. The deep, baritone voice on the other end of the line was the stern voice of authority: steady, unwavering. After listening to a description of the bag and its chilling secret, Titus denied owning such a piece of luggage. He then told Sturgis a provocative tale about his nineteen-year-old daughter, Frances, and her star-crossed relationship with a twenty-one-year-old man from Delton named Morris Newton.

On September 8, "Frankie" left a note under her dinner plate and disappeared. The wording of the note was cryptic, but Titus suspected that Frances was pregnant and had left town to avoid the stigma attached to an unwed mother.

Detective Sturgis did the math. The baby in the bag died at the age of six weeks. That placed the birthdate sometime in early November. Frances would have left Cloverdale in the third term of her pregnancy, at the point when she could no longer conceal her baby bump. Everywhere she went in the small village, she would a carry with her a tangible reminder of her premarital "sin."

Titus's voice wavered a bit when he explained that he didn't go to the police because he didn't want to shame his daughter or blacken her reputation in the community. Instead, he combed Cloverdale and Delton looking for Frances. He traveled as far as Grand Rapids, spending a weekend knocking on doors and showing people a photograph, but he could not locate her.

Sturgis knew where to begin searching. Women in trouble often went to the Salvation Army Rescue Home on Division Street for help.

At about the same time Ed Titus was describing his daughter's trouble, Morris Newton led Frankie by the hand into the Gothic, castle-like

Grand Rapids City Hall. For the past few hours, Newton had become melancholic. He spoke little and kept a straight face, which worried Frankie. This was the not the face of the man she had known and loved for the past four years.

Newton's glumness seemed to erode as they approached the office of the justice of the peace. The two lovers exchanged a smile as they stood in front of Justice Harry Creswell. The civil marriage ceremony would be a fresh start for the young couple.

They did not realize that, a few blocks away, Detective Warren Sturgis was hot on their trail.

Sturgis and an *Evening Press* reporter reached the Salvation Army Rescue Home after lunch on Wednesday, December 11.

Lena Higham, the head matron of the home, received the men in her office. The reporter flipped open his notebook and scribbled notes as Mrs. Higham described a "Frances Newton" who had applied for admittance to the home on October 24. The description matched that of the missing teenager from Cloverdale.

Two weeks later, on November 8, Frances gave birth to a baby girl she named Dorothea Newton. Each day, a man—Morris Newton, who presented himself as Frances's brother—came to visit. On December 3, Frances Newton checked out and left with her "brother."

Sturgis handed Higham a few garments he had found in the bottom of the valise.

She nodded. They belonged to Dorothea Newton.

From the Salvation Army, Sturgis traced Frances Titus and Morris Newton to a Division Street address where they lived for a short time before moving into an apartment at 132 Commerce.

Sturgis handed photographs of Frances Titus and Morris Newton to Mrs. Lackey, the landlady.

Mrs. Lackey studied the photographs for a few seconds. A wry smile spread across her face. She knew them as "Mr. and Mrs. Frank Johnson."

"Frank Johnson" was an affable, athletic specimen who had recently secured a job with the GR&I Railroad. He loved baseball and often spoke to Mr. Lackey about the Detroit nine.

"Mrs. Johnson" kept to herself, seldom emerging from her room. Mrs. Lackey thought her antisocial behavior stemmed from hours of sleepless nights. For weeks, the other tenants had complained about the wailing of a baby in the middle of the night. She assumed the Johnson baby suffered from colic.

Then, on Tuesday night, December 10, at about 8:00 p.m.—Mrs. Lackey remembered the time because she was cleaning up after dinner—the infant's crying stopped. She looked out the window and saw Johnson leaving with a large valise under his arm.

Sturgis cringed as he envisioned Morris smothering the child and sneaking out at night to toss his daughter's body into the Grand. That scenario would explain the sudden cessation of wailing, but Dr. LeRoy had ruled that Dorothea Newton either drowned or died of exposure. So a more likely scenario had Newton lining the case with the baby's clothes, gently setting his daughter on top of the makeshift mattress, tiptoeing to the edge of the river and watching as the perforated bag slowly sank. By jettisoning the baby clothes, Newton attempted to remove any tangible evidence of the infant's existence. The couple appeared determined to erase that short chapter of their lives.

According to Mrs. Lackey, Johnson returned sometime around 10:00 p.m. The next morning, just a few hours before Sturgis visited 132 Commerce, Mr. Lackey noticed the door to the Johnson apartment ajar, and he peered inside to discover that the couple had packed all their belongings and left without saying a word. Detective Sturgis now realized that he had missed "Mr. and Mrs. Johnson" by just a few hours.

Sturgis anticipated the couple's next move. From Commerce, he made a beeline for the courthouse. He didn't come away with the murder suspects, but he did obtain a copy of the marriage license issued on December 7. The bride-to-be gave her name as Frances Titus, age twenty, and the groom as Morris Newton, age twenty-three. Both listed their current residence as Grand Rapids, but with their "sins" washed away in the Grand River, Sturgis believed, they would go back home.

He guessed right again but experienced another, frustrating near miss at Union Station. A man and woman matching his suspects' descriptions purchased tickets on the Michigan Central train en route to Hastings, which departed at 3:45 p.m.

Sturgis failed to apprehend the Newtons, but he managed to piece together their movements from Tuesday through Wednesday afternoon except for a two-hour window on Tuesday night from 8:00 p.m. to 10:00 p.m.—the time frame of Dorothea Newton's murder.

It was already dark when the evening express coach pulled into Cloverdale at 5:25 p.m. on Wednesday, December 11. Frances and Morris strolled arm in arm across the platform. She beamed as he introduced her to friends and relatives at the station as Mrs. Frances Newton.

Frankie's brother, Edward Jr., yelled, "Hullo, Frankie!" She giggled like a schoolgirl.

Smiles turned to frowns when an *Evening Press* reporter asked them to step inside the station. "Outside," he wrote, "the brother waited patiently while this boy and girl were subjected to a questioning and in their effort to show a clean bill of health told several conflicting stories."

The reporter asked about the satchel found floating in the Grand. Frankie denied ever seeing it until the reporter read the inscription found etched in blue pencil. Then she remembered her father had sent it to her.

The lovers denied the existence of Dorothea Newton, but the newspaperman saw through the lies: "They were nervous and terribly confused when their own conflicting statements were arrayed in parallel and the absurdity of their efforts to conceal something made apparent."

Morris Newton yanked on Frances's arm, pulling her out of the station as she stood, silently staring at the *Evening Press* man. He pulled her all the way to his parents' house, but he could not run away from the accusations.

He had just about enough time to hang up his coat when the telephone rang. It was a *Grand Rapids Herald* reporter. Newton pressed the receiver to his ear and listened as the reporter rattled off the chain of evidence linking him to the baby's murder.

Newton's voice trembled as once again he denied everything. The couple, he insisted, hadn't left Cloverdale to hide evidence of their indiscretion. There was no Dorothea Newton and never had been.

As Morris hung up the receiver, he realized that the Delton sheriff would likely be on his way to the Newton farm. He turned to Frankie. "Here they come for me now," he said. "But they'll never take me alive."

Frankie followed him into the front parlor, where he dropped to his knees. She stopped. For a moment, she thought he was about to say a prayer until she noticed him reach for the shotgun leaning against the wall.

"Goodbye, Frankie, be a good girl," he said without turning to look at her and pressed the barrel against his chest.

The shot shredded Newton's heart and tore a gaping hole in his back. He fell face forward, a ring of blood forming as the warm liquid oozed from his body onto the floorboards.

Frankie stood frozen, not realizing that her hair and face were speckled with dots of her husband's blood and bits of his flesh.

Back in Grand Rapids, Detective Warren Sturgis purchased a ticket aboard the night train to Hastings. He planned to drive the rest of the way to Delton and bring in the couple for questioning. Now there was only one.

A translucent glaze of ice covered the steps leading into police headquarters on the morning of Thursday, December 12, 1907. The teenaged widow, clad in a black taffeta dress, clung to the arm of Warren Sturgis as she climbed the flight of stairs.

Sturgis handed her to the police matron, Charlotte Collier, who escorted her to a holding cell. A few minutes later, Prosecutor McDonald, followed by Chief Carr and Warren Sturgis, listened to her side of the story.

Allowed to eavesdrop on the interview, an *Evening Press* reporter described the nineteen-year-old murder suspect: "Dressed modestly in her gray coat, a dress of plain but good material, with her lustrous brown eyes looking forth frankly into the eyes of her questioner, she depicts the trustful, unsophisticated country girl."

Frances folded her hands in her lap and looked at Prosecutor McDonald. Her lips curled up at the ends to form a faint smile, and in a monotone unbroken by sniffles or sobs, she narrated the story of her love affair with Morris Newton.

Grand Rapids Police Headquarters as it appeared on a postcard dated 1906. *Author's collection.*

She described a fairy tale romance with her childhood sweetheart. Newton, considered an Adonis in Delton, was popular. As a result of his attention, fifteen-year-old Frances became the town's belle and an object of envy among the other girls.

Frances discovered she was pregnant in April. She did everything she could to conceal her condition, but by September, it had become impossible. To avoid embarrassment, Morris took her to Grand Rapids, where she gave birth to Dorothea in November.

Then, Frances explained, things began to go bad. After several sleepless nights caused by Dorothea's incessant crying, Morris wanted to get rid of their baby.

"Soon after my baby was born, my husband began to devise means to get rid of it," Frances explained. "He wanted to poison it. He said he would bury it in Cloverdale. I would not consent to this. Then he talked of throwing it in the river, and to this, also, I objected."

They finally agreed to leave their child on the doorstep of the Children's Home. "We had read of such things being done, you know," Francis said with a shrug, "and I thought perhaps they would care for her."

By Tuesday night, Morris had had second thoughts. He decided to leave the child on the doorstep of a cousin's house. At about 8:00 p.m., he took Dorothea away in a valise. "Be sure baby gets a good home," Frances called out as he left with the bag under his arm. Meanwhile, she packed their

Trains pull into the Union Depot train shed, circa 1900–10. *Detroit Publishing Company, Library of Congress.*

things. When he returned at about half past ten, they went to Union Depot, checked their luggage and spent the night at the Crathmore Hotel. The next morning, they made their relationship official at the courthouse.

That afternoon, Morris had appeared glum, not the man facing his happily ever after with his princess bride. He was clearly bothered by something, but he told Frances "he was not feeling well."

A few hours later, when the couple arrived at the Delton station and were confronted by the *Evening Press* reporter, she found out what was on his mind. He had betrayed her by taking their baby to the riverbank.

Frances paused. A smile spread across her lips. "He was good to me, and I love him." Her use of the present tense hinted at the possibility that Frances Titus Newton had not yet grasped the reality that her husband of twenty-four hours was dead.

The suspect appeared unaffected by her ordeal, but McDonald knew that the eyes don't lie. Frances's bloodshot eyes lacked the vitality of a person who had enjoyed a good night's rest. Bags under her eyes accentuated her high cheekbones, creating an eerie, skeletal visage.

It had all happened so fast. Within the past twelve hours, she had learned that her longtime lover had betrayed her by murdering their child, and she witnessed his suicide. The shock of the double tragedy apparently hadn't worn off yet. Carr worried about what would happen when it did. He ordered Charlotte Collier to spend the night in a chair outside of Frances's cell.

"With her nerves completely shattered and little more than a physical wreck as the result of the awful crime of infanticide," wrote a *Daily News* reporter, "Frances Titus Newton, victim of an ill-starred love, lies at police station on the verge of nervous prostration."

As the story became front-page news in Grand Rapids, the community of Cloverdale rallied around Frances. They viewed her as a naïve schoolgirl lured into a sinful relationship with the elder neighbor boy. Some even speculated that a childhood injury had left her with a fractured psyche. An *Evening Press* correspondent repeated the village gossip in a December 12, 1907 front-page story about the case:

> *Frances Titus when only six years old fell from the haymow of a neighbor's barn. When they picked her up the bones of the forehead were broken and crushed in against the brain. It was thought she would die, but the girl recovered under careful nursing and this injury had the result of making her at times hardly responsible for her actions. When laboring under excitement or anger it was often found necessary to restrain her and knowing this the neighbors who loved her unhesitatingly assert that whatever wrong she has done she is not to be held fully responsible.*

Locals were equally protective of their favorite son. Coroner LeRoy had jotted "Probably exposure" as a cause of death on Dorothea Newton's death certificate. They thus concluded that the baby was dead before she entered the water, an assumption that became the basis of a less sinister scenario for the baby's demise.

The apologists envisioned Morris Newton leaving his daughter on a doorstep, as he and Frances had agreed, but tragically Dorothea froze to death before she was discovered. Whoever found her deposited the valise in the river out of convenience or fear. Newton's suicide, they argued, resulted from a crisis of conscience triggered by having abandoned his daughter and inadvertently causing her death.

While understandably popular in Delton, this version ignored the fact that the bag was found only partially submerged, which meant that Dorothea could have died of exposure in the water.

The next morning—Friday, December 13, 1907—Ed Titus and W.W. Potter, an attorney from Hastings, arrived at Grand Rapids Police Headquarters.

While Potter met with Prosecutor McDonald and Chief Carr to review the case and attempt to talk McDonald out of pressing charges, Ed Titus trotted up the steps to the second floor.

Frances lay on the cot curled in a ball. When her father stepped into the cell, she sat up and bowed her head as if in prayer. Titus sat on the cot next to her, and she buried her head in his chest and sobbed. He felt her quavering against his chest.

After a few minutes of muffled crying, she lifted her head and attempted to talk, but nothing came out except mumbled ramblings that morphed into a series of shrill, banshee-like shrieks. Her cries were so loud, they echoed through the corridor and down the stairs to the first floor, where Potter was trying to talk McDonald out of charging Frances.

Ed Titus had just managed to hush Frances when Warren Sturgis appeared at the cell door. He motioned for Titus to join him in the corridor outside. Frances watched as the two men whispered. After a few minutes, Titus walked over to his daughter, grabbed her shoulders and pulled her to her feet. Sturgis wiped away a tear as he watched Ed Titus throw his arms around his daughter and embrace her. Friday the thirteenth had been a fortunate day for Frances Titus Newton. She was going home.

None of the investigators—including Carr and Sturgis—favored charging Frances with a crime. They believed that if Newton had thrown their child into the Grand, he did so without her knowledge.

The moment was captured in time by an *Evening Press* reporter: "While the news seemed to revive her considerably, yet the moments spent with her father seemed to bring the awfulness of the affair down upon her and she was changed from the girl to the sorrow stricken woman."

The *Evening Press* reporter ended his story of the tragic affair with a final dig at Morris Newton when he wrote that "she was only the ignorant, unsophisticated tool of the man she loved."

Too Much Time on Her Hands

The same day Frances Titus gave birth to Dorothea in Grand Rapids, a parole board considered Jennie Flood's case.

Not content to idle away her time in the Detroit House of Correction, Flood created a graphic spectacle to use as evidence of her innocence. She created a scale model replica of John London's death scene, complete with a likeness of London lying on the floor with a shattered skull.

Jennie Flood was not one to miss a detail, no matter how tiny. She recreated every aspect of the farmhouse kitchen as it appeared on April

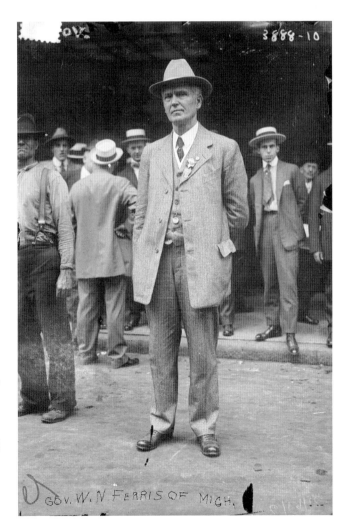

Woodbridge Nathan Ferris, governor of Michigan from 1913 to 1917. In his last few months as governor, he paroled a record number of convicts, including Jennie Flood. *Detroit Publishing Company, Library of Congress.*

21, 1903. Her model even contained the spots of blood and brain matter splattered onto the ceiling and walls, prompting one member of the parole board to characterize the miniature as the most ghastly exhibit he had ever seen.

It is unclear whether Flood's exhibit helped or hurt her cause, but the parole board denied her petition, and she went back to her House of Correction cell for the remainder of her life sentence.

Not everyone agreed with the parole board's decision. In 1916, Michigan representative Roy M. Watkins, convinced of Flood's innocence, pleaded to Governor Woodbridge Nathan Ferris for executive clemency. Watkins knew that Ferris had made a pledge that before he left office, he would release any inmate worthy of clemency.

Throughout December 1916, Ferris nearly ran out of ink issuing paroles, pardons and commutations for over four hundred prisoners. In the eleventh hour of his governorship—on December 29, 1916—he released fifty-two convicts, including lifer Jennie Flood. The pardon came with great controversy. An editorial in the *Detroit Free Press* accused Ferris of "grandstanding" and using his power of pardon to wipe away jury verdicts.

Nonetheless, Jennie Flood's life sentence came to an end after thirteen years behind bars.

8

THE USUAL SUSPECTS, 1921

Fiction writers would need no more than the actual facts [about the robbery]
*to weave a story possessing all the dramatic elements required by the most exacting
adventure magazine editors.*
—Grand Rapids Press, *March 29, 1922*

M onday, January 23, 1922, was a blustery day in West Michigan. Wisps of wind created miniature cyclones of snow swirls that danced across the sidewalk outside Grand Rapids Police Headquarters, where officers were on the verge of breaking one of the most sensational cases in the city's history.

The chair shrieked as Grand Rapids police superintendent Ab Carroll slid it across the floor toward his suspect, Leo Bolger. He sat down, folded his arms across his chest and waited for Bolger to begin his story. Since Carroll's days as a "turnkey" at the county jail, he had ascended to become the city's top cop—a position in which he earned a reputation as a stubborn cop who would bend a few rules from time to time to get the job done. Detective Thomas Blinston, who played a key role in collaring Bolger, slid into a chair next to his chief.

Detective Warren Sturgis stood against the wall and toyed with his wedding band. He never did have children of his own, but he did find love again. In November 1914, he married forty-year-old Musa Fuller.

Sturgis eyed Rose Finkelstein, who sat next to her live-in lover, her head bowed. The ordeal of their arrests had taken its toll on the pretty twenty-two-year-old. Deepening fissures spreading outward from the

Liquor bottles confiscated by Grand Rapids police. The notation on the back of the photograph reads, "Locked closet in office of A.B. Carroll, chief of police of Grand Rapids, Mich., containing bottles of many fluids of alcoholic drinks found on 'drunks.'" *Grand Rapids History & Special Collections, Archives, Grand Rapids Public Library.*

corners of her eyes hinted at periods of intense crying interspersed with restless nights.

For four months, Grand Rapids police tried without success to track down the bandits who held up the Michigan Exchange Branch of the Grand

Grand Rapids detectives in a group photograph, circa 1915. Five detectives seated in the front row played vital roles in breaking the 1921 bank heist. *From the left*: William Youngs, Chief Ab Carroll, Warren Sturgis, Thomas Blinston and Garret Doyle. *Grand Rapids History & Special Collections, Archives, Grand Rapids Public Library.*

Rapids Savings Bank on Grandville Avenue. The $14,000 heist led to the murder of two detectives, the discovery of an underground still and dozens of red herrings.

Leo Bolger—a thirty-year-old hood with a mop of black hair, deep-set eyes and a thin mustache—held the key to solving *the* crime of Prohibition-era Grand Rapids. Police nabbed him in Detroit, brought him and Finkelstein to Grand Rapids and lodged the pair in police headquarters.

Bolger took a deep breath, sighed and began:

> *Up to a few months ago, I had always been fooling around garages, doing garage work. Lately, I had been handling liquor as well as doing garage work; in fact, bootlegging was about all I did for a year and three months until I lost what money I had made. Then I went to work. I made quite a bit at the liquor game, made close to $12,000 out of it at one time, but I lost the money.*

During his career in the "liquor game," Bolger met "Mac," a fellow bootlegger who went by the name McFarland. McFarland drafted Bolger

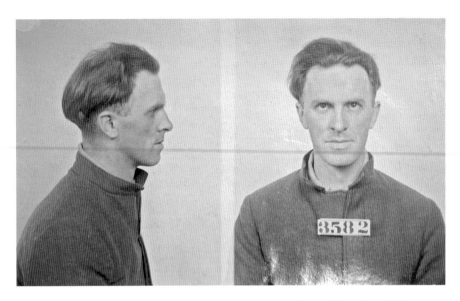

A state prison mug shot of Leo Bolger, taken after his sentencing in November 1922. *Courtesy Archives of Michigan.*

into what he believed was a liquor-smuggling job in Grand Rapids, but when they arrived, Bolger learned the job was really a bank heist.

> *I didn't meet the other members of the gang until shortly before the robbery, and I didn't know they planned a robbery when I started for Grand Rapids with them. I supposed they were going to carry booze, and if I'd known what they intended doing and what their record was, I wouldn't have had anything to do with them.*

By the time he learned their game, Bolger said, it was too late. "I didn't have the nerve then to back out, and so I saw the thing through." Bolger, a former cab driver, was tasked with driving the getaway vehicle.

The crew that held up the Grand Rapids bank, Bolger said, was led by a group of hardened criminals. "Mac" was the ringleader. Another member of the crew went by the name Bobby Walker. Bolger didn't know the names of the others. He only knew their nicknames: "Big Red" and "Pete." The crew viewed Bolger as an outsider and didn't entirely trust him, so he didn't know much about their past or their plans for after the Grand Rapids heist.

They initially planned a brazen scheme of three consecutive robberies. While the police hunted for culprits they assumed were on the lam, the gang would lay low for a while in Grand Rapids before hitting the second bank

A Stutz motorcar, 1920. *National Photo Company, Library of Congress.*

on Division Avenue. Then, a few days later, they would hit a third bank and leave town with triple the loot.

On November 30, 1921, the group, traveling in a stolen Buick, arrived in Grand Rapids. They rented a house on Weaver Street, and for the next week, they prowled the streets casing the targets and tracing escape routes. They made several practice runs until they had the timing down to just three minutes inside the bank. Meanwhile, "Mac" and Bolger returned to Detroit, where they stole a Stutz, which they planned to use as the getaway vehicle.

They picked their targets carefully. The Grandville Avenue bank was in an area not carefully watched by police. Just a few years earlier—in 1919—a crew had hit another bank just down the street. Local police cracked the case inside of a week. "Mac" wouldn't make the same mistakes.

The score was to take place on Tuesday, December 6, 1921, but then they learned that the bank would remain open on Wednesday evening, possibly due to the arrival of a cash shipment. So they planned the job for the next day.

Bolger would never forget that day; every detail was burned into his memory.

The hour hand pointed to 2:00 p.m. as three bank employees—two tellers and the manager—stood inside the cage and flipped through greenbacks, their backs to the front door, when the robbers burst in. They stood up sharply when they heard the command, "Put 'em up!"

"Don't turn around!" the robbers hissed as one of the tellers began to turn.

In the corner of his eye, the manager, R.A. Westrate, noticed a black Buick Six parked along the curb, the engine running.

"Keep 'em up!" the thieves barked as they marched, at gunpoint, the three employees and two stunned customers into the Director's Room at the back of the building. After forcing one of the tellers to open the vault, two men went to work inside while the third kept an eye on the five prisoners, who were lined up facing the wall.

"For the love of Mike," one of the customers pleaded, "make it snappy. We've been in here long enough."

"Shut up!" one of the bandits howled.

A few minutes later, the two men emerged from the vault with a sack full of banknotes totaling almost $14,000. One of the men pushed the prisoners into the vault. "Damn it, hurry!" he yelled as he kicked at Westrate's heels. He pressed his body against the heavy door, closing the five men inside.

It was four minutes past two o'clock. The thieves were in and out in less than five minutes.

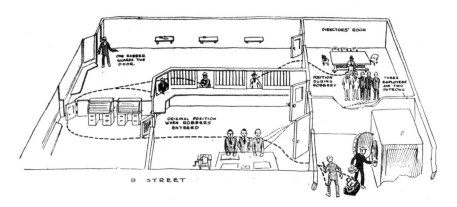

This sketch of the Exchange Bank robbery was published on the front page of the *Grand Rapids Herald* the morning after the robbery, December 8, 1921.

The plan was working perfectly—except, in mapping the getaway route, Bolger had failed to account for the railroad crossings. As luck would have it, they met a train at the Fulton Street crossing.

Bolger floored it, but when he realized he wouldn't beat the locomotive, he swerved in an attempt to avoid a collision. His split-second decision cost the crooks. Their Buick smashed into the front of the train.

Bolger remembered the crash in vivid detail:

> *The machine struck the train and locked somehow. We were dragged along—it seemed to me for two miles. It was only ten rods really, and when I realized what had happened I found myself clutching a bow on the top of the auto with one hand and a rail of the track with the other, the car being partly overturned.*

Bolger pulled himself out of the tangled wreckage and bolted. He ran as fast as he could before slipping into a nearby shed to catch his breath. He watched as, one by one, the other men emerged from the twisted car and moved down the street.

Railroad employee A.J. Gerard stopped his car and offered one of the men a ride to the hospital. The man's face was lacerated from shattered car glass, and Gerard noticed he carried a bundle under his arm. Instead of accepting Gerard's offer, the man turned and flagged down a passing Cadillac Touring Car.

The driver, Henry J. Gieger, stopped. To his shock, one of the men pointed a gun in his face. Climbing into the back seat, the carjacker ordered Gieger to turn around and pick up his companions. One of them got into the front seat and jammed a pistol in Gieger's ribs. "Drive like hell!" the man barked.

They sped a few blocks along Buchanan when the man in the front seat ordered Gieger to stop. He shoved him out of the car. Bolger, meanwhile, had watched the entire spectacle and ran to meet up with the gang. With Gieger lying by the curb, Bolger slid behind the wheel and gunned the engine. They continued along their planned route.

Two hopped out at the corner of Burton and College Streets. Another jumped out on Madison. At this point, Bolger dumped the Cadillac on Lake Drive in East Grand Rapids before returning to the planned rendezvous point: a bungalow on Weaver Street they rented from an unsuspecting landlady named Emma Horner.

At about eight o'clock on the evening of Wednesday, December 7, 1921, as the thieves began divvying up the loot in the bungalow's dining room, Detective Samuel Slater rapped on a door of A.J. Gerard, who lived directly across the street. With him was Special Officer Gerrit "George" Brandsma.

Gerard, who worked for the Pennsylvania Railroad, had witnessed the accident. After the bandits carjacked Henry Gieger, Gerard had briefly given chase before calling police and then returning to the crumpled-up car.

Surveying the wreckage, he found an overcoat, a .45 with three notches in the handle, a few handkerchiefs knotted into facemasks and a pair of silk stockings. When Geiger returned home that night and told his wife about the incident, she remarked that the coat he described resembled the type worn by the men who had recently moved in across the street. His mother-in-law, Margaret Brown, also noticed two men enter the house, one of them carrying a satchel that appeared to be heavy. Gerard became suspicious and called his old friend Ab Carroll.

Carroll recommended that Slater bring a team of five to Weaver Street, but Slater balked. They had received so many baseless tips that he wanted to take a look first.

As their car squealed to a stop in front of the Gerard residence, the lights in the bungalow across the street went out.

The investigators stood in front of the picture window and watched for any movement. "Guess we'll take a look," Slater decided after a few minutes.

Gerard, telephone in hand just in case, watched the scene unfold through his front window.

Brandsma knocked on the bungalow door while Slater waited behind him on the porch. The door opened a crack, and a face appeared. "What do you want?"

"We're from the police department, and we want to search the house," Brandsma replied.

"You can't search the house," the face snapped and began to close the door, but Brandsma wedged his foot in the jamb. Slater lunged forward and helped force the door open enough for his partner to reach inside the gap.

Brandsma grabbed the man by his neck and pushed his way into the living room. He made it a few feet into the house before two bullets slammed into his chest. A third hit him below the left ear, ripping through his brain before coming to a stop against his spine. He was dead when he hit the hardwood floor.

Outgunned, Slater turned for the street.

Two more shots, fired from the left side of the house, hit Slater in the midsection, tearing through his stomach and spinning him like a top. He pressed his hands against his stomach, warm blood oozing over his fingers, as he stumbled across the road. "They got me, oh God, they got me," he mumbled as he pulled himself up the front steps of the Gerard residence.

Gerard dialed the police. "The bandits have got them. Hurry!" He had just hung up the receiver when he heard a pounding on his front door. It was Detective Slater, who managed to whisper, "They got me," before collapsing on the frontrunner. "Get me a priest," he uttered.

A few minutes later, Gerard heard the roaring of an engine. He spotted five figures—four men and a woman—leave in what looked to be a Cadillac or a Stutz.

In Gerard's front room, eighty-two-year-old Margaret Brown knelt beside Slater, who groaned in agony. Gerard had called a priest, but Mrs. Brown

A group of police officers pose outside of Grand Rapids Police Headquarters in 1911. Sam Slater, who died during a shootout with bank robbers in 1921, stands fourth from the left. *Grand Rapids History & Special Collections, Archives, Grand Rapids Public Library.*

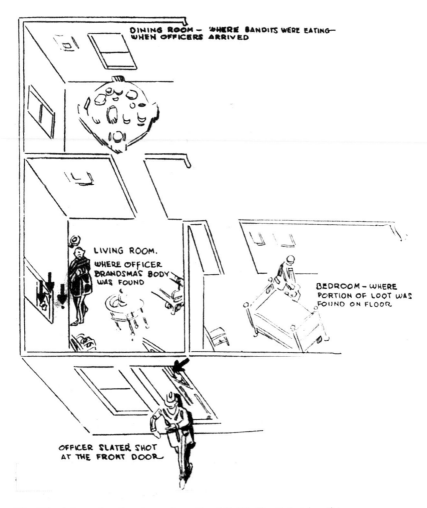

The "death bungalow," as drawn by a *Grand Rapids Herald* sketch artist.

didn't want to take a chance. She made the sign of the cross and began whispering the Act of Contrition. "Oh, my god, I am heartily sorry." She paused as Slater repeated the words, his voice a weak mumble. When Mrs. Brown finished, Slater lost consciousness.

Within minutes, quiet Weaver Street was buzzing with activity. Curious neighbors stood a respectful distance from the "bandit house" as police officers and reporters searched the bungalow for clues. Meanwhile, doctors at Butterworth Hospital fought to save Sam Slater's life.

Brandsma's body lay on the floor under the dining room window. He gripped a flashlight in his left hand; his right hand was in his pocket, his fingers clenched around the handle of his revolver.

In the bedroom, one of the detectives found three white shirts, each with the laundry tag still attached. One of the gang foolishly failed to remove the tags, which indicated that the man had his shirts pressed at a Detroit laundry. Despite reports describing a blond woman seen around the house, there were no women's clothes in any of the rooms.

Meanwhile, a full-scale manhunt had begun. Posses of ex-soldiers and inflamed citizens patrolled the streets while police cordoned off streets in an attempt to throw a net over the city.

They were on the prowl for five suspects. After interviewing the bank employees, Gerard and other neighbors, Carroll believed the suspects included four men and one woman. The *Grand Rapids Herald* described them:

> *No. 1, 40 years old, six feet in height, weighs 200 pounds and is dark complexioned. In the wreck yesterday afternoon he received cuts and bruises about the face.*
>
> *No. 2, 27 or 28 years old, five feet, seven inches in height, weights 150 to 170 pounds. Light complexion.*
>
> *No. 3, 21 years old, five feet, seven inches in height, weighs 150 to 170 pounds. Light complexion.*
>
> *No. 4, five feet, nine inches in height, slim, dark complexioned, with dark eyes. Yesterday he was the man driving the car.*
>
> *The woman seen about the bungalow is medium height, well built, 25 years old and blonde.*

The descriptions went to police stations in every major city throughout the Midwest. Within hours, leads began pouring into the Grand Rapids police station. One phone call from Jackson Police chief Don Hudson convinced Carroll that the chase for the bandits would soon come to an end.

Ab Carroll, flanked by Detective Blinston and Jackson chief of police Don Hudson, studied Claude Gidoney. With soft brown hair tinged by gray strands and glistening eyes that gave him the appearance of a dapper sophisticate, the suspect looked more like an accountant than a bank robber. But Carroll knew from years on the prowl that appearances could be deceiving.

Gidoney's arrest was the result of his association with a looker named Margaret Bacon. When Hudson had read the description of the woman seen around the Weaver Street house, he immediately thought of Bacon—a dishwater blonde in her twenties who lived in an apartment above the Billiard Hall on West Pearl Street in Jackson. Bacon's husband, Lester, was in the penitentiary serving fifteen to twenty-five for his part—driving the getaway car—in the robbery of the Farmers State Bank in Grass Lake on July 29, 1920, which culminated in the shooting death of Undersheriff Harry Worden.

Margaret Bacon, at five-foot-two and 130 pounds, had a curvaceous, well-built figure. Like the Weaver Street blonde, she had icy blue eyes and wore a blue hat and a black fur boa. Further, the car wrecked during the getaway was a Buick stolen in Jackson.

When Chief Hudson went to Bacon's apartment, he found Claude Gidoney, who fit the description of suspect No. 2. A search of Gidoney revealed a bankroll of $1,804 in crisp new twenties, fifties and hundreds.

Carroll envisioned a scenario in which Lester Bacon orchestrated or perhaps even planned the Grand Rapids robbery from his Jackson cell, but his hopes for a quick resolution to the crime ended when Gidoney provided a logical explanation. He and Margaret had gone on a road trip around the Midwest. He said he withdrew the cash from a bank in Niles.

A few quick phone calls verified much of Gidoney's story. It was just another dead-end in an exhaustive sequence of leads that had kept the phone in Carroll's office ringing off the hook.

While Carroll and Blinston returned to Grand Rapids, Warren Sturgis went east to Detroit, where he hoped to trace the laundry tags found on the shirts left in the Weaver Street house by one of the bandits.

On Saturday morning, December 10, 1921, family and friends crammed into the living room on Adams Street to pay their final respects to George Brandsma. His wife, Cora, and eldest daughters sat, arms interlocked, and quietly wept while the two youngest children—three-year-old Florence and fourteen-month-old Gerald—played a game of hide-and-seek among the black-clothed legs in the room.

Thirty-nine-year-old Brandsma was a relative newcomer to the Grand Rapids police force. He worked as a constable for a while, took a hiatus and returned in 1920. His murder left Cora and the children without means, but the directors of the Savings Bank vowed that the slain officer's kin would not become destitute. While the family grieved, they purchased the house occupied by the Brandsma family and prepared a deed for the widow. They also paid the funeral expenses.

At the same time, on Bates Avenue, Sam Slater's wife and three daughters sobbed as they looked through photo albums and family portraits. The twenty-four-year veteran cop held on for thirty-six hours, finally succumbing to his wounds on Friday morning.

Slater's career began in 1897, when he left his father's farm in Caledonia and became a police constable. He gradually worked his way up the ranks to special officer and, finally, detective.

The city mourned the two fallen officers. The department had lost a handful of cops in the preceding years to traffic accidents, but not since the shooting death of George Powers in 1895 had an officer been murdered in the line of duty.

Carroll, exhausted but as indignant as ever, remarked after the funeral, "They have done their part—their killing. Now we're going to do ours. It's going to be a long hunt—but it will be some hunt, I'm thinking."

On Saturday morning, December 10, 1921, the *Herald*'s front-page headline carried the sad news to residents: "Police Seek New Bandit Clues; Slater Dies of Bullet Wounds from Death Bungalow Gun Fire."

Local banks anted up a king's ransom for the cop killers: $10,000 for the gang or $2,000 for each member. The county kicked in another $1,000 and printed wanted posters and sent them out across the country.

Detective Garret Doyle slid the skeleton key into the front door lock and gently turned it until he heard a click. The Lincoln Avenue home, in a quiet neighborhood, seemed like a good place to hide a secret. Doyle, trailed by a half dozen volunteers, followed up a hot tip about the possible identity and location of the bandits on the evening of Tuesday, December 13. It was a long shot that any of the players remained in Grand Rapids, but Carroll couldn't afford to ignore any lead at this point. A week had elapsed since the robbery, but Carroll and his men had failed to identify, let alone collar, any of the bandits.

As soon as he slipped inside, Doyle sniffed the pungent odor of sour mash. He followed his nose to the basement, where he discovered two large copper stills and a pyramid of whiskey casks. The search exposed an underground distillery, but it was another dead-end in the hunt for the Exchange Bank bandits.

Two days later, police brought in an enigmatic woman who, they suspected, could have been the woman seen around the Weaver Street house. Carroll met her in his office.

"Just call me Pearl Button," she said with a flirtatious tone. "That's a pretty name." She grinned, which seemed to flex every muscle in her face.

Pearl was a mysterious figure. She attended the funerals of both Brandsma and Slater; she attempted to rent the bungalow on Weaver Street; and rumor had it that she frequented local banks, depositing large sums in bundles of small denominations. Suspecting her to be the woman involved with the gang of bank robbers, Carroll had her brought to his office for an interview.

This "woman of mystery," as the *Herald* called her, was Mrs. Jeane Hughes. She continued to smile as Carroll questioned her about the robbery-homicide and answered each question with the exaggerated intonation characteristic of a parent talking to a child. The tone chafed Carroll.

After an exhaustive grilling, it became clear that Mrs. Hughes had no connection to the bank robbers and played no role in the heist. She was released, but it would not be the last time "Pearl Button" would visit the Grand Rapids Police.

The sun had just begun its ascent on Sunday, January 22, 1922, when Carroll, Thomas Blinston and a squad of Detroit detectives lined up outside an apartment on West Grand Boulevard. It took a few weeks, but the Detroit detectives managed to trace the laundry tags to a taxi driver named Leo Bolger.

The building superintendent, flanked by Carroll and Blinston, knocked on the apartment door. One of the detectives stationed on the street below noticed a window curtain rise only to be snapped shut. Ten minutes later, Rose Finklestein answered the door.

Rose squealed when Carroll and Blinston brushed past her and raced to the bedroom, where Leo Bolger was fast asleep. Blinston pointed his .38 at Bolger's head while Carroll kicked him in the thigh. Bolger bolted upright and wiped the crust away from his eyes with the back of his hand. His eyes widened when he spotted Blinston's revolver.

"I expected it," Bolger said with an air of feigned indifference.

"Well, my boy, I guess we have you," Carroll said.

Bolger nodded. "I think so. It was those laundry marks. I was told they'd get me through them."

Before the Detroit authorities released Bolger into Carroll's custody, they dragged him in front of James Brickley, the victim of a smash and grab. Brickley fingered Bolger as the man who had robbed him of $6,000 that he was about to deposit in the bank.

On the train ride to Grand Rapids, Bolger began to talk. He agreed to give a full statement once they arrived at police headquarters.

Bolger paused before continuing his narration. He looked out the window of Carroll's office. Since he began that morning—January 23, 1922—the sun had crawled across police headquarters and began its descent in the west. The bare tree limbs swayed in the gentle breeze.

According to Bolger, "Mac"—a shadowy and violent figure—was the ringleader and the one who shot Brandsma. He knew "Mac" in Detroit as a bootlegger and thought his last name was McFarland, although he didn't know for certain because the shady character masqueraded under a dozen different aliases.

Bolger, however, insisted he only heard and didn't see the shootings: "I had the motor of the car running at the time. I went to go out, and I saw [Bobby] Walker come running out with his gun in his hand, saw him run around from a corner of the house. He said, 'Get your doors open, get ready to get out of here!'" Walker then ran to the front of the house and fired on Slater.

After the shootout on Weaver, the gang hightailed it out of Grand Rapids, managing to make it out just before roadblocks sealed the city. They went their separate ways, with Bolger returning to Detroit. Three days later, he used his take to rent the lavish apartment on West Grand Boulevard.

Bolger sighed and stared at Carroll for a few seconds. He shook his head and smirked in an attempt to appear cavalier, but he was unable to conceal the disgust that seeped out in the tone of his voice. "The others told me the police would catch me from those laundry marks. Every one of the others cut theirs out, even taking out the tailor marks in their clothes."

He massaged the bridge of his nose with his thumb and forefinger. He could go up the river for the long haul this time, and all because of a damned laundry tag. He remembered McFarland once say it was the little things that matter.

"It gets me how you can come down to my apartment and pluck me. There are only three persons who know I was in on the job. I'd give $1,000 to find out how you found me, how you came right down to the spot and got me."

"My man," Carroll said in the tone of a father scolding a child, "we were at your apartment on Saturday night, but you were not at home. You did not get in Sunday morning until two o'clock. We then decided to call in the morning."

"Well, I take my hat off to you."

Convinced that Rose Finkelstein was not the moll involved in the heist, Carroll ordered her release. She immediately rented an apartment in Grand Rapids so she could stay close to Leo.

Over the next two months, Carroll and his detectives checked over every aspect of Bolger's story. His knowledge of the thieves' identities was sketchy, but he gave detailed descriptions of the four men. Grand Rapids detectives studied rogues' galleries and consulted with prison authorities across the country, and by late March, their legwork had led to the positive identification of the bandit leader as Frankie "the Memphis Kid" McFarland.

Well known in the criminal underworld, forty-three-year-old "Mac" went by a variety of aliases. To various people at various times, he was the Memphis Kid, Paul Rogers, Paul Latimer, Arthur McMahon, George Conklin and others. His real name was Frank McFarland, a pool shark and a career criminal adept at staying hidden for long periods of time. His rap sheet included seventeen arrests for charges ranging from pickpocketing to grand larceny. He served time for robbery in Walla Walla, Washington; Los Angeles; and Omaha.

McFarland, Bolger said, had even bragged about a Council Bluffs, Iowa heist that climaxed in a shootout at a safe house. "Officers were turning the county upside down to find our bonds and money," McFarland bragged, "but we buried the swag, and it's still there."

The Memphis Kid had left tracks across the Midwest, but Carroll's men were always one step behind the shrewd criminal.

Carroll and Blinston were reasonably sure that Bobby Walker was a career criminal also known as Robert Leon Knapp, and they believed that "Big Red" was possibly "Big Red" Sloan—an alias of Nicholas Trainor, who was a known associate of McFarland and Knapp. They had no clue about the identity of "Pete." Even though Bolger did not name a female accomplice, opinions remained divided over whether the gang included a woman.

The case cooled off until late March, when McFarland supposedly turned up in New York under the alias Michael Campbell.

On Wednesday, March 29, 1922, "Michael Campbell" faced a magistrate in Whitehall, New York, charged with stealing train rides. Herman Bartholomew and Michael Blackburn, detectives working for the Delaware and Hudson Railroad, collared Campbell aboard a sleeper car en route to Canada.

While the magistrate sentenced Campbell to six months in Albany, Constable George Netto recognized his likeness from a wanted poster issued by authorities in Grand Rapids. He raced to the police station, snatched the poster from a bulletin board and ran back to the courtroom. Holding up the poster and glancing at Campbell, he concluded that Michael Campbell was really Frank McFarland, wanted for robbery and murder in Grand Rapids, Michigan.

Bartholomew and Blackburn went into a cell with Campbell. Thirty minutes later, their suspect was prepared to sign anything they put in front of him. They hadn't touched his hands.

He copped to the murder of Brandsma: "He [Brandsma] pounced on me. What was I to do? I shot him."

Campbell also explained his reason for confessing: "I have not been able to sleep. The thing has been on my conscience night and day. Every night when I went to bed, I could see the man I shot. He was always before me."

Carroll kept Bolger under lock and key and his story under wraps while police combed jail and prison records for McFarland and Walker. The complicated web of aliases made them difficult to track. By mid-March, authorities were no closer to finding the two shooters.

Then, on the evening of Wednesday, March 29, 1922, Ab Carroll received a titillating telegram from Upstate New York:

> *I am holding one Frank McFarland, whose description tallies with your circular of March 13. After considerable grilling and after being shown pictures, admits photo and also that after robbing bank he killed policeman who pounced on him. Wire quick full particulars covering killing. He was leaving for Canada when picked up.*
>
> H.A. Bartholomew, Sergeant D&H Police

That night, Carroll and Detective Warren Sturgis boarded an eastbound train. Carroll had his doubts. The hardened criminal described by Bolger would not crack so easily. Then again, Carroll thought, authorities across the Midwest were hunting for McFarland. Perhaps, ironically, he wanted to seek refuge in a New York prison by being arrested under the alias Campbell. While police pounded the pavement, he would enjoy three squares and a warm bed for a few months courtesy of New York State.

Campbell's confession made headlines in Grand Rapids. The *Grand Rapids Herald* loudly proclaimed the capture of McFarland on the front page of the March 30, 1922 edition under the headline "Ghost of Slain Officer Haunting Bandit Brings Confession."

Ab Carroll and Warren Sturgis reached Whitehall, New York, on Thursday evening, March 30, 1922. Both men felt a sense of excitement.

There was a spring in Bartholomew's step as he led Carroll and Sturgis to Campbell's cell, where the suspect lay on the cot with his back against the wall. Carroll's mouth dropped open when he walked into the cell. Michael Campbell was not Frank McFarland. There was a certain resemblance but not enough to warrant the trip from Grand Rapids.

Carroll asked Campbell to stand up. The prisoner groaned as he struggled to pull himself off the cot. Sturgis measured his height and compared it to McFarland's Bertillon card. They did not match.

Why, Carroll asked, would he confess to the crime? Campbell explained that Bartholomew and Blackburn had given him the third degree. They shot ice-cold water in his face, throttled him and "blackjacked" him. So, fearing for his life, he agreed to sign whatever they wanted. In fact, he had an alibi they had never bothered to check: he was in Port Arthur, Ontario, at the time of the Grand Rapids robbery.

The deflated detectives left the police station with their heads hanging. The spring in Bartholomew's step was gone.

Authorities immediately released Michael Campbell, but his ordeal hadn't yet come to an end. Washington County district attorney Wyman S. Bascom wanted to press charges against the railroad detectives. He convened a grand jury and sent for Campbell.

Detectives of the railroad, Campbell later alleged, attempted to prevent his testimony by kidnapping him and sending him to Canada, but Bascom's men intercepted him and safely escorted him to court. Based on Campbell's testimony, a jury convicted Bartholomew and Blackburn of second-degree assault. The court sentenced each man to a sixty-day jail stint and a $500 fine.

After the debacle in New York, the leads dried up, and the search for McFarland and Knapp went cold.

April showers meant trouble for several Grand Rapids couples. While Carroll and his crew searched in vain for McFarland and Knapp, back in Grand Rapids, Prohibition agents kept busy busting moonshiners.

"Dry agents" followed a tip to a home on Valley Street by John Ball Zoo. The homeowner, Ludwig Kulhawik, bragged to his neighbors that he had made over $40,000 running an illegal distillery.

When presented with a search warrant, Kulhawik refused to allow the officers through the front door, so they pushed past him. Meanwhile, Mrs. Alexandria Kulhawik raced to the bathroom, where she began dumping gallons of hooch into the toilet.

It took some looking, but eventually the agents found three stills installed in a hidden alcove under the basement staircase. Kulhawik managed to mask the strong odor of mash by venting the stills through his chimney flue, which allowed the couple to evade discovery long enough to make a small fortune with their illegal operation. In the raid, the cops confiscated thirty gallons of whiskey and a massive cache of raw ingredients, including fifty-seven cases of malt extract and nineteen barrels of mash.

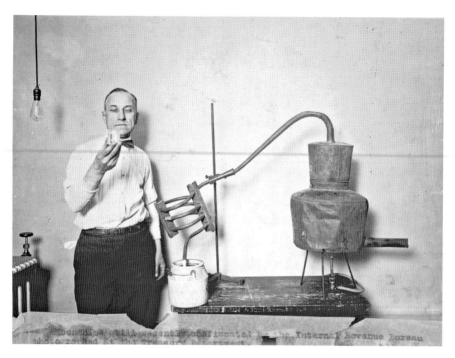

Above: A Prohibition officer displaying an illegal still confiscated during a raid. *National Photo Company Collection, Library of Congress.*

Left: A typical Prohibition-era whiskey still. *National Photo Company Collection, Library of Congress.*

Across town, on Shawmut Street, agents busted in on Sophie Roman, mother of seven by day and bootlegger by night. They found Roman's twenty-gallon still sitting in her kitchen, where she cooked up whiskey while her children slept. The fifty gallons of mash suggested that Mrs. Roman did considerably more than brew booze for personal use.

One of the city's illegal liquor rackets ended when a housewife found an empty bottle in the trash. The discovery put "Pearl Button"—one-time suspect in the Exchange Bank robbery—behind bars for a second time and, in the spring of 1922, in court.

Pearl Button stood and listened as the foreman announced the jury's verdict: guilty of "possessing and selling liquor." The trial emanated from the sale of a single bottle of whiskey to Frank E. Burns. When his wife, Eileen, discovered the bottle in her husband's possession and grilled him about its provenance, he confessed to purchasing it from Mrs. Hughes, who had rechristened herself with the curious name Pearl Button. That one bottle triggered charges against Pearl and her husband, Gilford T. Hughes, for violating Prohibition. Pearl faced the jury on April 5, 1922.

The key testimony in the brief trial, the story told by Frank E. Burns, convinced the ten men and two women in the jury box that Pearl engaged in a sort of liquor delivery service. Police heard talk about a female bootlegger who catered to an elite clientele, and this woman's description matched Pearl. They could find no solid evidence linking Pearl with an illicit trade in liquor until Mrs. Burns found an empty bottle in her trash bin and blew the whistle.

Frank Burns testified to purchasing alcohol from Mrs. Hughes. He said he did everything conceivable to keep his wife from discovering the bottle. He described a humorous cat-and-mouse game in which he kept moving the liquor from spot to spot in the house. At one time, he said, he hid it behind a pickle barrel. At another, he stashed it in the coal bin. His tragic error came when he finished it and threw the empty into the trash bin. Mrs. Burns sniffed out the whiskey bottle, boxed her husband's ears and swore out a warrant against Pearl Button.

A *Grand Rapids Press* reporter described the curious figure: "'Pearl Button' appeared undisturbed at the announcement of the verdict. A smile was her only response to a question as to what she thought of it."

Pearl seemed to enjoy her fifteen minutes of infamy when she spoke about her stage name:

> *I like the name "Pearl Button." I've had a good time since I was married four years ago at the age of 15. And I have had a good time in Grand Rapids. This certainly is a swell town. There are some real sports here. No matter what my name used to be before Chief Carroll tried to "pump" me, I'm now "Pearl Button," the galloping kid from Montreal.*

During Prohibition, people found clever ways to evade the dry laws. In this photograph, a woman playfully sweetens her cola with whiskey concealed in a cane. *National Photo Company Collection, Library of Congress.*

Pearl flirted with police and reporters alike when asked about an illegal river of whiskey flowing into Michigan: "Do you ask me if there is a booze channel from Canada? Well, you know I'm mum about such things—but if you tried you might guess a lot. And, anyway, I believe it would puzzle some officers to train an elephant in fresh snow."

Leo Bolger noticed the familiar silhouettes of Rose, his brother Dennis and a friend named Louis Smith outside his cell. From apartments on Ottawa Avenue, the three made daily trips to visit Leo in jail. Ever faithful, Rose typically brought a basket lunch to replace the jailhouse slop.

By Sunday morning, November 26, 1922, Leo Bolger was into his eleventh month behind bars in Grand Rapids. He tried to make the most of his small accommodations. A *Grand Rapids Herald* reporter described Bolger's cell as resembling "a prima donna's 'back stage' dressing room": "From the low steel ceiling to the concrete floor, the walls are bedecked with the photos of film stars and variegated magazine covers."

While Rose and Leo chatted, a team of detectives rifled through Finkelstein's apartment and the adjacent room rented by Dennis Bolger. They found $1,000 worth of booze in Bolger's room and telephoned Carroll, who sent Blinston and Sturgis to arrest the trio for violating the city's liquor laws.

The color drained from Rose Finklestein's face as Blinston grabbed her arm. She began whimpering.

A few minutes later, Carroll visited Rose in her new apartment: a cell on the first floor.

"Mr. Carroll—my God!" Rose protested in a whine cooked up with equal parts of shock, fear and indignation. "It's news to me."

Carroll felt a sense of déjà vu—except it was more than just a feeling. He had experienced this reaction from Rose Finklestein before. The discovery of the liquor cache was the last straw for Carroll, who had grown tired of the havoc caused by Leo's girlfriend.

The previous summer, she had become embroiled in what became known as the "Darling affair." In August, Carroll caught wind of a possible plot hatched by Rose and an ex-showman named Fred N. Darling. In exchange for busting Leo out of the city jail, Rose would—through Leo—feed him information about the whereabouts of McFarland, Walker and the others. Darling would then cash in on several thousand dollars in reward money.

The crafty Carroll had Rose followed. Police nabbed Rose and Darling during a meeting in Crescent Park. A pat down of Darling revealed a handgun and a hacksaw. In her signature whine, Rose denied all wrongdoing. Without enough evidence to make a case, Carroll reluctantly released Rose with the strong suggestion that she leave town.

Rose took Carroll's suggestion, but she just couldn't stay away from Leo. She returned to Grand Rapids, but since the Darling affair, Carroll didn't trust her, so he ordered his men to search her apartment while she was at the station visiting Leo.

She claimed ignorance about the thirty-five bottles uncovered in Dennis Bolger's room; in another cell, Bolger took responsibility. Dennis Bolger was headed to court, but once again, Carroll didn't have enough to charge Rose. Nonetheless, he now had the justification he needed to order Finklestein out of the city. This time, he made sure she left.

As 1922 came to an end and the Grandville Avenue robbery neared its one-year anniversary, Leo Bolger was the only one available to answer for the crime. And the newspapers had blasted him in front-page headlines, prompting Carroll to make a statement on the eve of Bolger's day in court, scheduled for Tuesday, November 28, 1922: "I've proved Bolger out in a thousand different ways, and I know he's telling us all he knows. One thing it seems to be very hard to get the newspapers and public to understand is that Bolger didn't know these other men before the robbery. He wasn't a pal of theirs."

Leo Bolger bowed his head and braced himself by leaning against Superior Court judge Leonard D. Verdier's bench. After Rose's incarceration, officials decided the time had come to rid the city of Bolger and his troublesome mistress. Rose had proved to be doggedly loyal, so wherever Bolger went, surely she would follow. Her indiscretion had hastened her beau's day in court.

Bolger listened to prosecuting attorney Cornelius Hoffius read the charge. For the first time, he showed some emotion by squinting. He didn't understand the legal terminology and wanted a clarification before he declared his guilt.

"It's just plain bank robbery, Leo," Hoffius said, his voice soft but firm.

Verdier knitted his eyebrows and peered over the top rim of the pince-nez sitting midway down his nose. The judge's steely gaze unnerved the prisoner, who nervously shifted his weight from one foot to the other. He tried to keep the cool façade he had maintained throughout his incarceration and chomped on a piece of gum.

"Whatever you do, judge," Bolger pleaded, "don't put the rest of the gang in the same prison with me if they're caught. If you do, it'll mean my life."

Judge Verdier shook his head:

> *You have admitted that you are guilty of bank robbery while armed and you are also guilty, at least of assisting in the crime of murder, and cold blooded murder at that. In the absence of a statute authorizing capital punishment which, in my opinion, is the only sort of a punishment which should be inflicted in a case of this kind, there is only one thing to do and that is to confine you where you can never commit such a crime again. The sentence of the court is that you spend the remainder of your natural life in the state prison at Jackson.*

Verdier smirked. "I regret that there is no capital punishment in this state for the crimes of this type," he said sharply. "If there were, I would sentence you to death."

Bolger dropped his head further until his chin touched his chest. Verdier continued, "Since there is not, I shall send you to Jackson prison for the remainder of your natural life." He tapped his gavel. To Bolger, it sounded like a hammer hitting an anvil.

The Bolger brothers would travel to Jackson on the same train. The day before, Judge Verdier had sentenced Dennis Bolger to six months for transporting liquor.

The hunt for one of the suspects—Nicholas Trainor—ended in a residential garage on Gilpin Street in Denver, Colorado, on January 14, 1923.

Denver detectives, assisted by FBI agents, pulled open the garage door to discover a black Buick perforated with bullet holes—the getaway vehicle in a shocking daylight heist that had taken place a month before.

At about 10:30 a.m. on December 18, 1922, a black Buick pulled up alongside the Federal Reserve truck outside the United States Mint in Denver, Colorado. Three men jumped out of the car, and while two of them scared guards by firing their shotguns in the air, the third man bagged up $200,000 in five-dollar bills.

Hearing the gunfire, a small army of Mint guards raced to the truck and began to fire at the thieves, strafing the Buick with bullets. In the ensuing firefight, one of the guards was killed, and one of the thieves took a round in the cheek before speeding away. Despite an exhaustive manhunt, the thieves eluded the long arm of the law.

One month later—on January 14, 1923—investigators received a hot tip that they would find the bullet-riddled getaway car in a garage on Gilpin Street in Denver. The frozen body of the thief injured during the shootout lay slumped over in the front seat. He turned out to be Nicholas Trainor, aka "Big Red" Sloan.

It was also live by the gun, die by the gun for the Memphis Kid. Details were sketchy, but Grand Rapids detectives learned that he took a bullet and died in a firefight following another bank heist out west.

Carroll crossed off another name from his list of suspects when Robert Knapp went to prison for bank robbery on an unrelated charge.

Despite the tentative identification of Sloan as "Big Red," Ab Carroll and his crew continued their hunt for both "Pete" and "Big Red." The most promising lead in three years came in 1925 following a shootout between a farmer and the culprits who had just robbed the State Bank of Millburg.

Thomas Blinston chatted with Berrien County sheriff Frederick Franz for a few minutes before approaching his quarry. It had been over three years since the 1921 robbery, but Blinston hoped to find the missing suspects in the Berrien County Jail. He came to obtain photographs of bank robbers Edward Summers and Frank King, two men in a five-man gang that had held up a bank in Millburg a few days earlier, on Saturday, February 21, 1925. Twenty-five-year-old Summers, a seasoned bank robber, matched the description of "Pete." His fellow thief, thirty-one-year-old Frank King, matched the description of "Big Red."

Franz waved his arms in the air in his animated description of the shootout, during which farmer Oscar Smith peppered the getaway vehicle with a sawed-off shotgun. The thieves took shelter in a barn south of the Indiana border, near New Carlisle, and prepared for an all-out gunfight until a South Bend cop threatened to torch the place and the suspects surrendered. Terrified of retribution from the bandits' friends, Franz purchased the first Tommy gun in Berrien County.

Summers groaned as he noticed Franz and Blinston push their way through the mob of curious onlookers crowding the corridor outside the cells. During the firefight, Summers took a load of buckshot in the face. He sat on a cot with bandages covering his forehead and right eye. His left eye was swollen to a slit, and the strafing buckshot sandblasted his face, leaving it a red, pulpy mass.

King was in even worse condition. He lay in his cot writhing in agony. A slug had shattered his kneecap.

Blinston ignored King and turned to Summers. "How're you doing, Pete?"

"I'm not Pete," Summers retorted. "And I have never been in Grand Rapids in my life." He frowned and stared at Blinston for a few seconds with his one good eye.

Summers sighed. "But I can't blame you. We're hooked, and it is good policy to hang everything you can on us—so go to it—and good luck."

Blinston left the jail with a pair of photographs that he planned to show local residents who had come into contact with the bandits who robbed the Grandville Avenue Bank four years earlier.

Even writers for the *Grand Rapids Press* seemed buoyed by the news. The front-page headline for February 25, 1925, read, "Brandsma-Slater Murders in 1921 May Be Avenged."

The crafty detective arranged a photo lineup by placing mug shots of the five Millburg robbers side by side. One by one, a parade of witnesses studied the pictures.

They could not agree. A grocer who sold vegetables to the gang fingered Summers as the man who answered to "Pete," but Mrs. Horner—the owner of the "death bungalow" on Weaver Street—wasn't so certain.

"If I saw any of them, it is this man," she said as she tapped the photograph of Edward Summers. "If it is not the man who was in the bungalow on the day of the rental, he closely resembles him. Of course, it is a long time ago, and this man seems to have more hair as I remember. The bandages may change his appearance, but he certainly looks like one of the two men I saw."

Leo Bolger would have the last word. When Blinston brought the suspects' photographs to Marquette State Prison, Bolger dashed all hopes with a quick shake of his head.

Nonetheless, King and Summers would join Bolger, who by 1925 had been relocated to Marquette to serve life sentences for bank robbery.

Bolger never mentioned the presence of a woman, but police continued to seek a possible female accomplice. Bobby Walker's girlfriend, Margaret Perry, alias "Indian Rose" Walker, was a prime suspect. For over a decade, they searched for Indian Rose but could not manage to locate her. The search reached a dead-end in the woods outside Balsam Lake, Wisconsin.

Early on the morning of March 7, 1932, passing motorists saw a cloud of black, acrid smoke pouring from the woods. They followed tire tracks for about fifty yards when they came across a Buick engulfed in flames with two bodies sitting upright in the back seat. With handfuls of snow, they doused the fire.

The charred remains belonged to two women who had been shot to death, their faces melted by nitric acid and their bodies burned into charred, twisted shapes. A singed piece of hotel stationery led detectives to a hotel in St. Paul, where they discovered the two women had stayed as "Margaret Perry" and "Margie Perry," sisters from Chicago. Despite the fire, investigators managed to lift a set of fingerprints, which led to the positive identification of the women as Margaret Perry and Sadie Carmacher, a prostitute and one-time cellmate of Perry's.

Perry, it appeared, chose to blackmail the wrong men. She knew the identities of the gang who had pulled a heist in Cambridge, Minnesota, and attempted to use that information to squeeze hush money from the thieves. The two women were last seen leaving a St. Paul hotel in the company of a known underworld figure named Jack Peifer, who, authorities surmised, murdered the women to protect his rackets.

With the murder of Margaret Perry—the last suspected accomplice in the Exchange Bank robbery—the case officially reached a dead-end. "Pete," whoever he was, remained officially unidentified.

The only one to do time in Michigan was the driver, Leo Bolger.

Bolger's life sentence came to an end in 1932 with a surprise denouement.

On December 17, Governor Wilber Brucker gave the lifer a break after Bolger help to foil an attempted breakout of the state penitentiary at Marquette.

Using guns smuggled in tins of chicken, four inmates attempted to shoot their way out of the prison on August 27. Their escape attempt began in the infirmary, where Bolger worked as an orderly. They shot prison physician Dr.

A.W. Hornbogen in the chest, killing him instantly. Bolger took a bullet in the shoulder. Warden James P. Corgan was also wounded in the ensuing fracas.

Responding to pleas from Hornbogen's widow and Corgan, Brucker reduced Bolger's sentence to sixteen to thirty years. With time off for good behavior, Bolger walked out of prison that winter, a free man.

The final word in the 1921 bank caper came from an unexpected source: the Denver police. In 1934—twelve years after the infamous Denver Mint heist—the Denver police released a statement officially closing the investigation into the robbery, which at the same time provided some sense of closure for Grand Rapids investigators.

According to Denver chief of detectives Albert T. Clark, the gang contained seven members, including Nicolas Trainor, aka "Big Red" Sloan; Harvey Bailey, serving life in Alcatraz on a kidnapping conviction; Jim Clark, serving life for an Indiana bank robbery; Frank McFarland; Robert Leon Knapp (alias Robert Burns and Robert Walker); Knapp's common-law wife, Margaret Perry (alias Margaret Burns and "Indian Rose" Walker); and "Big Red" Sloan's lover, Florence Sloan (alias Florence Thompson).

Both McFarland and Walker, Clark confirmed, were dead. Vengeance for the murders of Slater and Brandsma would not belong to the citizens of Grand Rapids, after all.

The identities of "Big Red" and "Pete" remain unsolved mysteries.

IN THE END:
THE EARLY LAWMEN OF GRAND RAPIDS

George Powers, Samuel Slater and Gerrit "George" Brandsma died with their boots on, but the other crime fighters featured in this volume did not. They continued to fight the good fight, most of them living well into their golden years.

Detective Jerry Darr, who played a critical role in tracking down Mary McKendrick's killers, died of heart failure on June 10, 1903. He was fifty years old.

In the fall of 1903, Detective Sherman G. Jakeway checked himself into Maple Roads sanitarium with throat cancer. His six-month battle with the disease ended on March 15, 1904—just about a year after Califernia "Jennie" Smith went to prison—when he died at the age of forty.

In 1909, a horrific accident involving an electric streetcar—by 1892, electric power had supplanted horsepower—ended the thirty-seven-year career of the police department's most senior member, Detective Cornelius Gast. Racing for Union Depot, Gast tried to jump onto a moving car. He missed the handrail and was dragged over the brick street. Agonizing injuries to his back, head and neck forced him to retire from the force that same year. He died in 1912 at the age of sixty-eight.

Joseph U. Smith—who, along with Sherman Jakeway, nipped William Lane's scheming in the bud—was appointed chief of detectives in 1910. He served in that capacity until his death of pernicious anemia on June 7, 1914, at age fifty-five.

After twenty-two years on the job, Garret Doyle retired as Grand Rapids Police detective in 1923. Three years later, his son Beriram died at the age of nineteen from an infection of the brain. The morning of Beriram's funeral, fifty-five-year-old Doyle collapsed and died of a massive heart attack.

Albert A. ("Ab") Carroll served as superintendent of police throughout the Roaring Twenties and beyond. He retired from the force in 1936. He suffered a heart attack and died at home on June 25, 1941, at the age of seventy-five.

Warren W. Sturgis outlived his second wife, Musa. He died a widower on January 22, 1947, at the age of seventy-eight.

Six weeks later, on March 6, 1947, Sturgis's fellow detective Thomas Blinston passed away at the age of seventy-three.

These hardboiled cops are gone, but as key figures in the story of early law and order in Grand Rapids, they are not forgotten.

BIBLIOGRAPHY

BOOKS

Baxter, Albert. *History of the City of Grand Rapids, Michigan.* New York: Munsell & Co., 1891.

Etten, William J. *A Citizens' History of Grand Rapids, Michigan; with Program of the Campau Centennial, September 23 to 26, 1926.* Grand Rapids, MI: A.P. Johnson Co. for the Campau centennial committee, 1926.

Goss, Dwight. *A History of Grand Rapids and Its Industries.* Vol. 2. Chicago: C.F. Cooper & Co., 1906.

Lawson, John Davison. *The Adjudged Cases on the Defences of Crime.* Vol. 6. San Francisco: Bancroft-Whitney Company, 1892.

Manual of the Police Department of the City of Grand Rapids, State of Michigan. Grand Rapids, MI: C.M. Loomis & Co., 1885.

Michigan Report of Proceedings of the Advisory Board in the Matter of Pardons for the Year Ending December 31, 1902. Lansing, MI: Robert Smith Printing Co., 1903.

Michigan Reports: Cases Decided in the Supreme Court of Michigan. Vol. 109, *March 24 to June 30, 1896.* Chicago: Callaghan & Co., 1898.

R.L. Polk & Co.'s Grand Rapids Directory, 1895. 23rd ed. Grand Rapids, MI: Grand Rapids Directory Company, 1895.

White, Arthur S. *Incidents in the Lives of Editors.* Grand Rapids, MI: A.S. White, 1920.

BIBLIOGRAPHY

NEWSPAPERS

Buffalo (NY) Courier
Grand Rapids Daily Democrat
(Grand Rapids, MI) Daily News
(Grand Rapids, MI) Evening Leader
(Grand Rapids, MI) Evening Post
(Grand Rapids, MI) Evening Press
Grand Rapids Herald
Grand Rapids Morning Telegram
Grand Rapids Press
(Grand Rapids, MI) Telegram-Herald
(Grand Rapids, MI) Times

ARCHIVES

Archives & Regional History Collections. Western Michigan University, Zhang Legacy Collections Center, Kalamazoo, MI.

City (of Grand Rapids) Archives and Records Center. Grand Rapids, MI.

Collections of the Public Museum of Grand Rapids, Grand Rapids, MI.

Grand Rapids History and Special Collections Department. Grand Rapids Public Library, Grand Rapids, MI.

State Archives of Michigan. Lansing, MI.

DOCUMENTS

Death Certificate for Bertha Van Norman, September 24, 1902. File No. 936. County of Kent, City of Grand Rapids, State of Michigan Department of State, Division of Vital Statistics.

Death Certificate for Calpernia [*sic*] J.S. Smith, March 29, 1904. File No. 1399. County of Wayne, City of Detroit, State of Michigan Department of State, Division of Vital Statistics.

Death Certificate for Dorothea Newton, December 10, 1907. File No. 785. County of Kent, City of Grand Rapids, State of Michigan Department of State, Division of Vital Statistics.

Death Certificate for Gerda Sturgis, January 6, 1904. File No. 16. County of Kent, City of Grand Rapids, State of Michigan Department of State, Division of Vital Statistics.

BIBLIOGRAPHY

Death Certificate for John London, April 21, 1903. File No. 127. County of Kent, Village of Ada, State of Michigan Department of State, Division of Vital Statistics.

Felony Record Book #10 (September 30, 1899–November 7, 1904). City of Grand Rapids, MI; p. 135, entry 10938 (Viola Stockard); p. 148, entry 11258 (Thomas Stockard); p. 171, entry 11676 (Minnie Brown); p. 171, entry 11677 (Myrtle Abbey); p. 172, entry 11678 (Lizzie Davis); p. 172, entry 11679 (Emma Rogers); p. 173, entry 11823 (Jennie C. Smith). City (of Grand Rapids) Archives and Records Center, Grand Rapids, MI. Community Archives and Research Center, Grand Rapids, MI.

Marriage Record of John Smalley and Cora Brown, March 13, 1893. Record No. 26. Return of Marriages in the County of Isabella for the Quarter Ending December 31, 1893, p. 319.

Marriage Record of Maurice Newton and Frances Titus, December 7, 1907. Record No. 1768. Return of Marriages in the County of Kent for the Quarter Ending December 31, 1907, p. 231.

Mug Shot Book #1 (1897–1915). Grand Rapids Police Department. Collections of the Public Museum of Grand Rapids, Grand Rapids, MI. Community Archives and Research Center, Grand Rapids, MI.

The People of the State of Michigan v. Califernia J. Smith. County of Kent in the Superior Court of Grand Rapids. File #2197, January 1903. Archives & Regional History Collections, Western Michigan University, Zhang Legacy Collections Center.

ABOUT THE AUTHOR

An aficionado of history with a dark twist, Tobin T. Buhk loves to poke around the closets, crawlspaces, basements and back alleys of history. He explored the dark side of the Civil War in *True Crime in the Civil War* (Stackpole Books, 2012); unearthed the truth behind Michigan's original Lonely Hearts Killer in *The Shocking Story of Helmuth Schmidt* (The History Press, 2013); probed the motives of Mary McKnight, the Michigan Borgia, in *Michigan's Strychnine Saint* (The History Press, 2014); and revealed the shocking murder-for-profit plot of Arthur Warren Waite in *Poisoning the Pecks of Grand Rapids* (The History Press, 2014).